The Christmas Tree Ship

Other Books by Cris Kohl and Joan Forsberg:

Dive Southwestern Ontario! (1985)
Shipwreck Tales: The St. Clair River (to 1900) (1987)
*Dive Ontario! The Complete Guide to Shipwrecks and
        Scuba Diving in Ontario* (1990)
Dive Ontario Two! More Ontario Shipwreck Stories (1994)
Treacherous Waters: Kingston's Shipwrecks (1997)
The 100 Best Great Lakes Shipwrecks, Volume I (1998)
The 100 Best Great Lakes Shipwrecks, Volume II (1998)
TITANIC, The Great Lakes Connections (2000)
The Great Lakes Diving Guide (2001)
Diver's Guide to the Kitchen (2003)
Shipwreck Tales of the Great Lakes (2004)
Shipwrecks at Death's Door (2008)
Our World--Underwater, The First 40 Years (Editors; 2010)

Maritime History Documentaries by Cris Kohl and Joan Forsberg:

Shipwreck Tales of the Great Lakes (2009)
Great Lakes Shipwrecks of the World Wars (2009)
Tales of Great Lakes Shipwreck Pairs (2009)
The Shipwrecked Whalebacks (2009)
Deep Shipwrecks of the Great Lakes (2009)
Shipwrecks at Death's Door (2010)
Exploring Canada's Great Lakes Shipwrecks (2010)
Thirteen Shipwrecks: The Great Lakes Worst Maritime Disasters (2011)
Shipwrecks off Whitefish Point (2011)
Shipwreck Tales of Chicago (2012)
TITANIC, The Great Lakes Connections (2012)
The War of 1812 on the Great Lakes (2012)

The Christmas Tree Ship

CRIS KOHL
AND
JOAN FORSBERG

The Christmas Tree Ship

Published by
Seawolf Communications, Inc.
West Chicago, IL
USA

Cover Designs: Cris Kohl and Joan Forsberg

Printed in Canada

FIRST EDITION

5 4 3 2 1

FRONT COVER ARTWORK: Detail of "Sailing into Eternity," a dramatic painting of the schooner *Rouse Simmons*, by Eric Forsberg. See www.ForsbergArt.com

HALF TITLE PAGE IMAGE AND TITLE PAGE BACKGROUND IMAGE: Detail of an archival photo of the schooner *Rouse Simmons* underway in Sturgeon Bay, Wisconsin. Courtesy of the Door County Historical Museum.

BACK COVER IMAGES (TOP TO BOTTOM): The schooner *Rouse Simmons,* departing with a deck load of lumber in 1912, framed in a 1912 Christmas card (Kohl-Forsberg Collection); Capt. Herman Schuenemann (The Christmas Tree Ship Historic Marker, Thompson, MI); the bow of the *Rouse Simmons* shipwreck in 165 feet of water (Photo by Cris Kohl).

TABLE of CONTENTS

❄   ❄   ❄   ❄   ❄   ❄

ACKNOWLEDGEMENTS

We extend special thanks to the following libraries and institutions:
National Archives, Great Lakes branch at Chicago, Illinois
Chicago Maritime Society, Chicago, Illinois
Door County Historical Museum, Sturgeon Bay, Wisconsin
Center for Archival Collections, Bowling Green State University, Ohio
Runge Collection, Milwaukee Public Library, Milwaukee, Wisconsin
Rogers Street Fishing Village Museum, Two Rivers, Wisconsin
Chicago Christmas Tree Ship Committee, Chicago, Illinois
von Stiehl Winery, Algoma, Wisconsin
Northern Illinois University, DeKalb, Illinois
College of DuPage, Glen Ellyn, Illinois
University of Windsor, Windsor, Ontario

In addition, we are thankful to the following individuals:
Eric Forsberg, talented maritime and *Rouse Simmons* artist
Glenn Longacre at the National Archives, Great Lakes branch, Chicago
Bob Graham, Center for Archival Collections, Bowling Green State University, Bowling Green, Ohio
Dr. Gerald Thomas and David Metzger, Chicago Maritime Society
Capt. Joseph McGuiness, U. S. Coast Guard Cutter *Mackinaw*
Tim Juhl for technical assistance
Kent Bellrichard, John Steele, Steve Radovan, Jim Brotz, and George West, early Great Lakes shipwreck hunters
Dr. William Ehling (grandson of Capt. Herman Schuenemann) and family
Dave Truitt, Rochelle Pennington, Fred Neuschel, Ruth Fleswig Gibson, Lee Murdock, Joyce Hayward, Dave Mekker, Tom Pakenas, all fellow advocates and promoters of the Christmas Tree Ship story

INTRODUCTION

She sits, cold and alone, at the bottom of Lake Michigan. Now surrounded by darkness, her last glimpse of sunlight was a century ago. The *Rouse Simmons*, in her heyday as the Christmas Tree Ship, bringing pines from the north woods to Chicago, shone with warmth and joy, but now she is bedecked only with her sad cargo of skeletal Christmas trees. Reaching her tragic end in the frigid, violent waters off Two Rivers, Wisconsin, the lost Christmas Tree Ship of 1912 became legend.

There are few Great Lakes shipwrecks that have attained "legend" status. The *Griffon*, the first shipwreck on the upper Great Lakes, is the most searched-for vessel, and the *Edmund Fitzgerald*, the most famous modern shipwreck and the subject of a popular song, is known worldwide. Helmed by "Captain Santa," the *Rouse Simmons* was such a source of joy and celebration that her loss affected thousands of people, and the story, even 100 years later, continues to move us.

We have long been fascinated by the legend of the *Rouse Simmons* and have researched the history of the ship and her times in great detail. This year, on the 100th anniversary of her loss, we wanted to commemorate the event by adding to the body of knowledge of this often-told tale to honor the ship, the family and the legend.

At the end of the 1800's on the Great Lakes, fragile, aging sailing ships were being replaced by new, mighty, steam-powered vessels and, by 1909, the busy harbor of Chicago had been moved a few miles south to the port of Calumet. The familiar sight of ships lining the Chicago River was no more. So the once-a-year arrival of a three-masted schooner festooned with lights and thousands of Christmas trees was a glorious sight at the river for Chicagoans eager to begin their holiday festivities. The arrival of the Christmas Tree Ship in Chicago to mark the beginning of the Christmas season was akin to the dropping of the ball in Times Square today to signal the beginning of a New Year. Chicago families looked forward to this rare and special occasion that had become a treasured tradition, full of excitement to buy their perfect Christmas tree from the jovial Herman Schuenemann, known as "Captain Santa."

Many years later but not really far removed from the *Rouse Simmons* story, our family, too, always eagerly anticipated the Christmas season with its attendant happy traditions and memories, especially the selecting and decorating of our Christmas tree. We so loved the Christmas tree that we put up a tree in every room to bring joy to every corner of our home. After all, with Cris' German and Joan's Swedish heritage, it seemed as though the scent of balsam and fir was in our blood. The giving of presents was a highlight for all, but especially for the children. It didn't matter whether the gifts were simple or elaborate, store-bought or home-made, because they were given from the heart with love, and that was what really counted. When she was a little girl, Joan asked her mother, "Is there really a Santa Claus?" Her mother smiled, hugged her, and softly replied, "I believe in Santa Claus. Santa is the spirit of loving and giving."

Captain Herman Schuenemann could have just sold the trees in a simple business transaction without the warmth he brought to that cold, Chicago River dock, without becoming "Captain Santa." But he was a believer, too. He risked everything each year to bring this special kind of happiness to the families of Chicago until 1912 when the *Rouse Simmons* could not survive the Lake Michigan storm. The ship and crew were gone, but the legend was born.

Cris Kohl and Joan Forsberg
High Lake, 2012

Dedication
We dedicate this book to our children,
Lara, Jennifer, and Geoff,
our sons-in-law, Juan and Dan,
and our grandchildren, Mark, Jason, and Lauren,
who always show us that
Christmas is all about love.

ONE

The Heritage of Christmas Trees

The tradition of Christmas trees as symbols of a religious holiday did not always exist in North America. Originating in the 16th-century German states, the idea of bringing a real tree into one's home and decorating it with colorful adornments took some time -- about 300 years, in fact -- to catch on elsewhere.

Trees such as oaks (long known for their great strength) and evergreens (hailed for their ability to stay green throughout even the most severe winters when other trees appeared to die) were held in pagan veneration by many of Europe's pre-Christian tribes. These attributes and early beliefs formed the foundation of the modern-day "Christmas tree."

But decorated evergreen trees were first used in, or just outside, Christian churches in northern Germany, usually as the "tree of paradise" prop in a "miracle play" given on December 24th each year. During the Renaissance, few people knew how to read, so the only way many of them could learn about the Bible was by watching actors dramatize biblical episodes throughout the year in short skits called miracle plays. At that time, December 24th was the designated day in the Christian calendar to commemorate Adam and Eve, so evergreen trees were decorated with apples (to symbolize the forbidden fruit in the Garden of Eden) and flat wafers (representing the Eucharist, or the Body of Christ) hanging from their boughs. In fact, the actor portraying Adam usually carried this decorated evergreen tree through the town with his troupe just prior to their performance.

This prop must have left a lasting impression, because even after the miracle plays ceased to be performed, people in Germany arranged for their own "tree of paradise," which they clearly associated with Christianity by now calling it a *Christbaum* (*"Christ Tree"*). As early as 1531, the public market place in the Alsatian city of Strasbourg (then part of Germany, now part of France) had vendors selling evergreen trees for Christmas.

According to German religious folklore, Christian Reformist Martin Luther (1483-1546) set up a small *Christbaum* with lighted candles in his home in the year 1536, but no historical evidence exists to verify this claim, which was made more credible to the general public by an 1845 painting by artist C. A. Schwerdgeburth depicting Luther and his family seated around such a tree (see page 33). Prints of this painting were widely circulated in the 19th century.

Upper-class Lutheran families most frequently set up Christmas trees in their households, while many German Roman Catholics initially viewed this as a Protestant custom associated with Martin Luther, preferring instead to set up Christmas cribs, or nativity scenes, in their homes. But the Catholics eventually embraced the Christian *Christbaum* concept as being acceptable, despite outcries from their priests, whose tolerance, if not actual acceptance, took longer to develop. The *Christbaum* was also seen as a strong expression of the Teutonic culture, including its touted German *Gemütlichkeit*, meaning cheerful mood, personal peace of mind, and a social mixture of food, drink and music. It was not until the Franco-Prussian War of 1870-1871 that the German Catholics and Protestants found a unifying agent for *Christbaum* acceptance. Ironically, it came in the form of the German military, which, significantly, decided to place Christmas trees in its many army barracks and military hospitals, in both Germany and occupied France.

Historic evidence suggests that predominantly the aristocracy and the well-to-do in Germany set up Christmas trees in their residences in the 17th and 18th centuries. Decorations consisted mainly of edible items, such as apples, wafers, cookies, nuts, and gilded candies, as well as paper roses symbolizing the Virgin Mary. One of the first references to a tree decorated with lit candles appeared in a 1708 letter from Liselotte von der Pfalz, who, recalling her privileged German childhood in the 1650's and 1660's, wrote,

> **...Tables are fixed up like altars and outfitted for each child with all sorts of things, such as new clothes, silver, dolls, sugar candy, and so forth. Boxwood trees are set on the tables, and a candle is fastened to each branch....**

In Johann Wolfgang von Goethe's 1774 novel, *Die Leiden des jungen Werthers* (in English, *The Sorrows of Young Werther*), which established his literary career and has been called the world's first "bestseller," his heroine, Lotte, describes a *Christbaum* decorated with fruit, candy,...and lighted candles.

The English writer, Samuel Taylor Coleridge, was in Germany for Christmas in 1798, and wrote this about his experiences there:

> **...On the evening before Christmas Day, one of the parlors is lighted up by the children, into which the parents must not go; a great yew bough is fastened on the table at a distance from the wall, a multitude of little tapers [candles] are fixed to the bough, but not so as to burn it till they are nearly consumed, and coloured paper, etc., hangs and flutters from the twigs. Under this bough the children lay out in great order the presents they mean to give their parents, still concealing in their pockets what they intend to give each other. Then the parents are introduced, and each presents his little gift; they then bring out the remainder one by one, from their pockets and present them with kisses and embraces. I was very much affected. The shadow of the bough and its appendages on the wall and arching over the ceiling made a pretty picture....**

The edible items on a *Christbaum* were usually left in place until January 6th, known as Epiphany, or Twelfth Night, the date commemorating the arrival of the Magi, or Wise Men, at Bethlehem. Then these items were picked off, or shaken out of, the tree and eaten. In the 1800's, small gifts gradually replaced many of the edibles placed on a Christmas tree.

The German Christmas tree tradition spread to neighboring countries in the late 1700's and early 1800's, first adopted by the aristocracy, since several royal houses were connected by marriage. Countess Wilhemine of Holsteinborg reportedly introduced Denmark to the Christmas tree in 1808, about the same time it reached Sweden. In 1816, when Austria was a part of the German Confederation and a half-century before it became the main part of the Austro-Hungarian Empire in 1867, Princess Henrietta of Nassau-Weilburg set up the first Christmas tree in Vienna. The Duchesse d'Orléans introduced the Christmas tree to France in 1840.

In England, several members of the royal family occasionally set up Christmas trees beginning in the early 1800's. King George III and his German wife, Queen Charlotte (Charlotte of Mecklenburg-Strelitz), for example, enjoyed a decorated tree for Christmas, 1800.

Their 13-year-old granddaughter, the future Queen Victoria, at Christmas, 1832 -- five years before she became queen -- wrote in her diary,

> **...After dinner we went upstairs. We went into the drawing room near the dining room. There were two large round tables on which were placed the trees hung with lights and sugar ornaments. All the presents being placed around the trees....**

But a Christmas tree was not, at that time, a regular annual custom among British royalty. In 1840, at the age of 21, Queen Victoria married her cousin, Prince Albert of Saxe-Coburg and Gotha, and in 1841, after the birth of the first of their nine children, the queen decided to annually embrace her husband's German tradition of setting up and decorating a Christmas tree. For their 1848 Christmas edition, England's popular weekly newspaper, the *Illustrated London News*, published a full-page drawing of Queen Victoria, Prince Albert, and several of their children gathered around a decorated Christmas tree. Due to the popularity of the queen and her royal family, the British quickly became a nation of imitators, thanks to the power of the print medium and this one influential piece of artwork (see page 34).

In North America, the decorated Christmas tree was introduced in Canada in 1781, when a regiment of German soldiers from the Duchy of Brunswick protected the British colony of Quebec against possible attack by the Americans during the Revolutionary War. Documentary evidence shows that General Friedrich Adolf Riedesel and his baroness wife entertained their Christmas guests at their residence in the town of Sorel with a Christmas tree decorated with fruits and candles.

A popular story tells of the pro-British German troops at Trenton who were surprised by George Washington and his soldiers in 1776 during the War of Independence while the Hessians were celebrating around a decorated Christmas tree, complete with lit candles. However, documentary evidence to prove this story is lacking. Meanwhile, the town of Easton, Pennsylvania, claims to have had the "first Christmas tree in America," set up by German settlers in 1816, but again missing documentation. Well documented is an account of a Christmas tree erected and enjoyed in 1821 by one Matthew Zahm in Lancaster, Pennsylvania.

The Christmas tree custom received some early literary assistance on two continents. In 1844, famous children's author Hans Christian Andersen from Denmark wrote a fairy tale called "The Fir-Tree." In the United States, the publication of a children's book called *Kriss Kringle's Christmas Tree* in 1845 in the United States also helped spread the holiday tree concept. England's most famous Christmas story author, Charles Dickens, who produced a classic tale in 1843 when he wrote "A Christmas Carol," surprisingly never included the Christmas tree in any of his books, instead writing about it only once in a magazine article published in 1850 in which he stated,

> **I have been looking on, this evening, at a merry company of children assembled round that pretty German toy, a Christmas tree. The tree was planted in the middle of a great round table, and towered high above their heads. It was brilliantly lighted by a multitude of little tapers [candles]; and everything sparkled and glittered with bright objects. There were rosy-cheeked dolls, hiding behind green leaves; and there were real watches (with movable hands, at least, and an endless capacity of being wound up) dangling from innumerable twigs; there were French polished tables, chairs, bedsteads, wardrobes, eight-day clocks, and various other articles of domestic furniture (wonderfully made in tin) perched among the boughs, as if in preparation for some fairy housekeeping; there were jolly, broad-faced little men, much more agreeable in appearance than many real men -- and no wonder, for their heads took off, and showed them to be full of sugar-plums; there were fiddles and drums; there were tambourines, books, work boxes, paint boxes; there were trinkets for the elder girls, far brighter than any grown-up gold and jewels; there were baskets and pin cushions in all devices; there were guns, swords and banners; there were witches standing in enchanted rings of pasteboard, to tell fortunes; there were teetotums, humming tops, needle cases, pen wipers, smelling bottles, conversation cards, bouquet holders, real fruit, made artificially dazzling with gold leaf; imitation apples, pears, walnuts, crammed with surprises; in short, as a pretty child before me delightedly whispered to another pretty child, her bosom friend, "There was everything, and more." This motley collection of odd objects, clustering on the tree like magic fruit, and flashing back the bright looks directed towards it from every side -- some of the diamond eyes admiring it were hardly on a level with the table, and a few were languishing in timid wonder on the bosoms of pretty mothers, aunts, and nurses -- made lively realisation of the fancies of childhood; and set me thinking how all the trees that grow and all the things that come into existence on the earth, have their**

wild adornments at that well remembered time....

In the 19th century, German and Scandinavian immigrants to the United States and Canada, perhaps a tad homesick for some of their Old World customs, brought their Christmas traditions with them, despite suspicions from various churches that this was a heathen custom.

What gave a huge boost in popularity to the Christmas tree in the United States, however, owes its success to that full-page, 1848 *London Illustrated News* print of Queen Victoria's family gathered around a Christmas tree. An American engraver procured a copy of it, made some changes to "Americanize" the artwork, e.g. he removed the queen's crown, lengthened Prince Albert's hair, expanded his shaggy sideburns, eliminated his mustache and the royal banner across his chest, and changed the style of many of the tree's ornaments, and published it in the

popular *Godey's Lady's Book* in 1850 in the USA. This new image represented the typical American family. The American reaction, while not as strong as the British one had been, still advanced the introduction of the Christmas tree to the general population.

In the early and mid-1800's, families wanting a Christmas tree bundled up warmly and set off with an ax or a saw into the nearest forest in the often fierce weather of early or mid-December, made a selection, cut the tree down and took it home to be set up and decorated with homemade ornaments. Before long, enterprising entrepreneurs made life easier for anyone seeking a holiday tree.

The first documented U.S. Christmas tree lot appeared on a New York City sidewalk in 1851 when a lumberjack named Mark Carr, from the Catskill Mountains 80 miles to the north, sold cut trees to city residents who had little or no access to forests. Carr, knowing

The "Americanized" version of England's royal family and tree. Compare this with the original artwork on p. 34. (KOHL-FORSBERG COLLECTION)

that there were many German families in New York City, had help from his two sons in cutting the Christmas trees and hauling them on two ox-sleds to the village of Catskill Landing on the Hudson River, where the evergreens were loaded onto a steamboat and transported to New York City. There, at the busy Washington Market, Carr paid a silver dollar to rent a strip of sidewalk at the corner of Greenwich and Vesey Streets, and began to sell his trees. His business boomed. He quickly sold out.

Mark Carr returned the following year with even more evergreens, and experienced the same amount of good fortune. Fifty years later, one of his sons was still taking a load of Christmas trees to sell in New York City -- amidst hundreds of other tree vendors! Sales had so rapidly escalated that 200,000 trees were sold at New York City's Washington market in 1880.

The 14th president of the United States, Franklin Pierce (1804-1869), has been denounced as one of the country's worst presidents for numerous reasons. For example, a Democrat from New Hampshire, he sympathized with slave owners and the South, and arranged for Kansas to be admitted to the Union as a slave state. When his presidency (1853-1857) neared the end of its term, his own party denied him the nomination for re-election! At age 48, he had become the youngest president the country had ever seen, the first one born in the 19th century, and the first one to hire a full-time bodyguard as a result of his many unpopular policies.

But Franklin Pierce also, in 1856, became the first president to celebrate Christmas with a decorated tree set up in the White House.

Pierce may have set up a Christmas tree in the childless White House out of a genuine concern over his wife. They had had three sons, all of whom died in childhood, the oldest at age 11 just before Pierce became president. His wife sank into a deep depression. Pierce thought that a Christmas tree might "snap" her out of her debilitating melancholia. It apparently did not. She died in 1863, and Pierce lost his lifelong battle with alcoholism in 1869 when he died of cirrhosis of the liver.

Although the first White House Christmas tree was set up in the 1850's, it was slow in becoming an established tradition there. Decades later, the press reported in late December, 1889, during Benjamin Harrison's presidency, that "...There was a Christmas tree at the White House for the first time in so many years that no one can recall a similar event."

Not to be outdone, the next president, Grover Cleveland, in 1896 set up a White House Christmas tree -- the first with electric lights!

Theodore Roosevelt, president from 1901 to 1909, an early conservationist aware that half of the USA's timber had already been removed, refused to have a Christmas tree in the White House, limiting the celebrations to gift-filled stockings hanging from the fireplace. His children enjoyed their aunt's Christmas tree.

In the first decade of the 1900's, frequent shortages of Christmas trees for sale in the larger cities became acute, and many families ended up having to do without one. These shortages spurred on the first productions of artificial Christmas trees.

Conservation methods were introduced, mainly the "thinning out" of evergreen forests rather than their "total leveling," and evergreen tree farms by the thousands sprang up on rocky pastures and other land ill-suited for farming, since these conditions proved perfect for coniferous tree growth. It took, on average, ten years to grow a perfect-size Christmas tree, and reforestation on an annual, rotating basis where evergreen trees had been cut proved efficient.

The end of the turmoil in the United States caused by the Civil War (1861-1865) brought about a general improvement in the national mood, an emotional situation that compelled more and more people to celebrate Christmas in new, imaginative ways, including the setting up of trees in their homes. Increasing numbers of European immigrants displayed increasing examples of how they celebrated Christmas in the Old Country. These pleasant customs proved contagious.

In the mid-1800's, many North Americans saw their very first Christmas tree in their church, community hall, hospital, mission, school or Sunday school (the American Sunday School Society was an early and huge supporter of the Christmas tree tradition), often years before they placed one in their own home. Other popular public venues for viewing larger-than-average, magnificently-decorated Christmas trees were the many German clubs and German beer halls found in most cities in the USA and Canada.

The decorations on these Christmas trees also became very important. Glittering tinsel strands called "icicles" -- thin strips of silver foil -- first appeared in 1878 in Nuremberg, Germany, and rapidly made their way to North American markets.

Shiny, glass Christmas tree ornaments, brought to North America by Europeans for the first time in the early 1860's, soon replaced some of the original fruit, candy, and older ornaments made from paper, wax, and tin on the tree. Glass ornaments became increasingly popular by the late 1800's, but they were very fragile and broke easily, and, because most of these beautiful creations were made in a mountain village in Germany named Lauscha, the costs were high, even more expensive than most of the German tin ornaments had been. But these European glass ornaments were desired in North America, and F. W. Woolworth in 1890, when he had only 13 stores in his rapidly-growing chain in the United States, ordered 200,000 glass balls from Lauscha. They sold out quickly.

In 1914, with the start of World War One and an Allied embargo on German products, North American supplies of Christmas tree ornaments soon ran out. Attempts by U.S. companies to reproduce the high-quality German glass balls met with failure, and after the war, Germany easily regained the North American Christmas tree ornament market.

In the late 1930's, with Europe again on a collision course with war, American wholesalers searched for a way to make glass Christmas ornaments in the USA. A number of Lauscha glassblowers had, over the previous two decades, immigrated to America, and many of them worked for the glass company at Corning, New York. In December, 1939, 235,000 Corning-blown Christmas tree ornaments were shipped to F. W. Woolworth's stores. After the Second World War, the production of Christmas tree ornaments in the USA increased sharply.

In the Christmas tree tradition, candles originally represented Christ as the "Light of the World." Today we can only imagine the vintage, 19th-century setting and the haunting beauty of many, tiny dancing flames on an indoor evergreen tree casting moving shadows in an otherwise dark room, plus the thrill of entranced children viewing this fairy-tale-like scene with wide-eyed wonder.

But candles were very dangerous, and many people were injured or killed when their Christmas trees accidentally caught on fire from the open flames.

To reduce the fire hazard, miniature oil lamps, with the flame protectively enveloped in a small glass mantle, were invented in 1887. However, by that time, a totally new form of lighting made its appearance, and it involved electricity.

American inventor Thomas Edison (1847-1931), in the late 1870's, produced the first commercially practical incandescent lightbulb, and for Christmas, 1882, one of his employees hand-wired a number of lights to be used on a Christmas tree. The last two decades of the 1800's saw increased development in this exciting new method of lighting a Christmas tree. But extremely high costs left electric lighting within the grasp of only the wealthy (since adding electric lights to a tree in 1890 cost the equivalent of $2,000 today!)

Miniature oil lamps for Christmas tree safety were patented in 1887.
(KOHL-FORSBERG COLLECTION)

A company called General Electric had purchased Edison's rights and his lightbulb factory in 1890, and by 1901 it tried to reduce the cost of electric Christmas tree lights. But strings of lights did not yet exist, and the individual wiring of each light proved complicated as well as pricey -- too much so for the average family. In 1903, the first "string" of 28 electric lights appeared on the market, priced at $12.00 -- which in 1903 was the average person's salary for a week. And faulty strings of electric lights still caused tree fires! Affordable strings of electric Christmas tree lights were finally developed in the late 1920's, but the problem of one burned-out bulb shutting down the entire string was not solved until several decades later.

In the first decade of the 1900's, postcards, which had been introduced to American society at the 1893 Columbian Exposition in Chicago, experienced an immense surge in popularity, particularly the colorful, German-made Christmas postcards depicting Christmas trees (see pages 36 and 39).

Christmas trees also entered the realm of music, but the English lyrics to the song, "O Christmas Tree," mean something different in the original German. With the German lyrics written in 1824 by Leipzig composer Ernst Anschütz, combined with a melody attributed to a 16th-century traditional folk song, "O Tannenbaum" literally means "O Evergreen Tree" in English. The song originally had nothing to do with Christmas and everything to do with truth and faithfulness represented by fir trees, but the lyrics were anglicized to "O Christmas Tree" in the early 1900's when the song was used in North America as a Christmas carol. Incidentally, the German word for Christmas tree is *Weihnachtsbaum*, not *Tannenbaum*.

By 1900, an estimated 20% of American homes erected an ornamented tree for Christmas, and its base became the repository for yuletide presents, replacing the earlier gifts decorating the tree and gift-filled stockings on the fireplace mantel.

Today, about 85% of American homes set up and decorate a Christmas tree for the holiday season. Despite the fact that many of these trees are artificial, and that today's volume of Christmas gifts has far outgrown the size of a hung stocking (or, for that matter, even the space at the base of a tree), a decorated Christmas tree still exhibits and retains a special family and holiday significance.

TWO

Chicago's Christmas Tree History

In the Great Lakes region, with its perfect climate for growing vast coniferous forests, ripe candidates for indoor yuletide beautification grew by the millions in the 19th century. Despite this fact, the joys of decorated Christmas trees remained alsmost exclusively the domain of European immigrants until the 1860's. It has been suggested that pious Yankees, already viewing German newcomers with disdain due to their proclivity for beer, looked with equal suspicion upon their old world Christmas tree custom.

And Chicago had an enormous German/European population in the latter half of the 19th century.

Why did Chicago need to import Christmas trees from northern locations? The enormous city actually sits at the point where the prairies begin, and where

THE CHRISTMAS-TREE.

The very large German and Scandinavian segments of Chicago -- a city which grew rapidly to become the largest on the Great Lakes -- imported a few of their Old World customs, including the family Christmas tree tradition.　(KOHL-FORSBERG COLLECTION)

the topography and soil conditions are not at all supportive of vast forests of coniferous flora, such as those existing in Wisconsin, Michigan, Minnesota, Ontario, Ohio, and upstate New York. The "prairie port" of Chicago had Lake Michigan at its doorstep, and the vast, mostly treeless prairies at its back. What little evergreen growth the Chicago area had been granted by Mother Nature was cut and utilized in the frontier days of the white man's settlement in the early 1800's.

European immigration to the United States and Canada flowed like a never-ending oil gusher beginning in the mid-1800's, and the new arrivals who came from Germany and Scandinavia particularly found Christmas tree hunting increasingly challenging while scavenging the outskirts of Chicago and Milwaukee for a small fir tree that they could cut, take home, and decorate.

In the 1850's, the Nordic Christmas tree tradition in Chicago's private homes was limited to newly-arrived but ambitious Europeans and a few of Chicago's wealthiest residents.

Fortunately, Christmas trees also found their way into Chicago churches and other institutions at that time. Here is a sampling of Chicago newspaper accounts in mid-19th-century (the original spelling, punctuation and grammar are retained):

> **Three hundred and seventy-five children, belonging to the Taylor Street Mission School, were made happy for a time yesterday afternoon, by a feast of good things, provided for them at their school by their benevolent and philanthropic teachers....**
>
> **Two "Christmas Trees" had been prepared by the teachers, from the branches of which were suspended a bag of candy for each of the 395 [sic] children. Eleven turkeys were divided among this hungry little multitude, and as much good biscuit and butter, apples and other good things as all could eat or carry away....**
>
> *-- Chicago Daily Tribune,* December 31, 1857

> **The ladies of the Third Presbyterian Church...will have a Christmas tree, filled with fancy and useful articles, suitable for Christmas presents,...**
>
> *-- Chicago Press and Tribune,* December 21, 1858

> **The Annual Christmas Dinner for the Orphans, will be...at the Protestant Orphan Asylum...the children will have a Christmas tree, and Mr. Dye will be present to sing with them....Those having donations, either for the dinner or Christmas tree, are requested to send them to the Asylum....**
>
> *-- Chicago Press and Tribune,* December 21, 1859

> **...The plan comprised an arrangement with Santa Claus to furnish every child of the Sabbath Schools connected with the [Wabash Avenue M. E. Church] a present, and the order was filled to the letter.**
>
> **A pair of stout evergreens were loaded with a burden that taxed all their sturdiness. Such toys; such dolls "with real hair" and eyes that would shut; such Noah's arks,...The mission of Christmas Eve was never better exemplified than on this occasion.**
>
> **...When the presents were distributed what a scene it was. Every child got some token from the tree, and the teeming branches shook down also more than one rich gift for an adult, some lady or gentleman present thus slyly and kindly remembered by a friend....**
>
> *-- Chicago Press and Tribune,* December 26, 1859

Chicago's churches and schools in the 1850's were responsible for creating thousands of children's very first fond memories of a Christmas tree. The custom at that time was to decorate the tree with hundreds of small gifts that would be distributed, often by a man in a Santa Claus costume, to the excited celebrants. (KOHL-FORSBERG COLLECTION)

...A very pleasant thing for the "young folk" was the Christmas Tree of the Wabash avenue Methodist Sunday School. The room was most tastefully decorated with the thick hanging evergreens, and two large trees hung full from floor to ceiling with the gifts which Santa Claus in full costume, not omitting the jingling sleigh bells, dispensed to the waiting expectants. The children were glad and joyous as youth always is upon occasion, and old hearts felt young again for the time. We are glad that this Christmas tree has become a permanent institution with the managers of this school, and think that others would not err in following their example....

-- *Chicago Tribune,* December 27, 1860

Next Friday evening it is proposed to have a Christmas Tree at the City Mission, for the Sunday school children. As yet, a large tree stands bare of everything but its evergreens, which is an emblem of immortal love and immortal life.... [The] little ones... will gather there in expectation of dolls, books, knives and candies. The tree stands at 96 North Franklin street, quite cheerless. Mr. Tuttle can welcome all who will remember his little flock.

-- *Chicago Tribune,* December 24, 1861

...Last evening, Christmas trees were erected in almost every house, and the Christ-child smiled benignantly above the gleaming tapers which spangled the gift-laden boughs. This morning thousands of little stockings, pendent to bed-posts, will be plethoric with the donations of the wrinkled little

old man from the far North,...

-- Chicago Tribune, December 25, 1862

In the early 1860's, Chicago newspaper articles about Christmas were often tinged with the justified sadness reflecting a nation in the midst of a Civil War. Thinking of loved ones fighting on battlefields far from home was the most common sentiment, but occasionally a burst of bitter anger found its way into print:

> **...The holiday season is at its height. The shops glitter with their shining treasures.... The confectioners' windows are bowers of sweets, the odors shaken down from the boughs of Christmas trees are in all our homes. Of a verity, were a lean and hungry denizen from the rebel capital to stray into our streets at this season, he might well believe he had died, and by some mistake gone to a better place than any rebel dying in his great sin of rebellion deserves to find.**

-- Chicago Tribune, December 31, 1863

At that same time, some newspaper writers expressed feelings of guilt about the materialistic pleasures in which Chicagoans indulged during the year's main religious holiday season, particularly during a time of civil war. In early January, 1864, one journalist calculated that the people of Chicago spent $340,000 for the celebration of the holidays -- an enormous sum of money at that time -- and subdivided that figure into seven categories: $150,000 for silver plate and jewelry of all kinds; $30,000 for toys; $25,000 for books, photographic albums, "&c"; $15,000 for pianos and other musical instruments; $10,000 for furs; $10,000 for confectionary of all kinds; and finally, $100,000 for "miscellaneous," which included clothing, millinery, and dry goods (and presumably, without naming them, "knives").

There were, however, money-raising benefits for the poor in Chicago, including, in mid-December, 1864, one "for the benefit of the Freedmen" [former slaves], which included the sales of "2,500 evergreens, just the thing for Christmas trees and parties." But whether the term "evergreens" in this context meant 2,500 individual boughs or 2,500 complete trees is not known. That number of complete trees would have signalled a high degree of Christmas tree popularity in Chicago.

At the end of 1864, with the Civil War's end in sight, the tone in Chicago became less tense and more relaxed:

> **There was hardly a happier sight in Chicago during the festivities of Christmas than was seen on Saturday last at the "Nursery and Half Orphan Asylum" on Michigan street....**
>
> **There was a Christmas tree adorned with toys, dolls and cornucopia, and tables loaded with cakes and good things, and plenty of nice books also, and all that could make children happy....**
>
> **Every child received a present according to its preference. Some wanted dolls, some wanted horses, some wanted knives, some wanted wagons, some wanted flags, some wanted books, all wanted candies and cakes, and all received just what they desired.**
>
> **It was pleasant to see their glee, and it was even pleasanter to know that there were generous hearts among our people willing and glad to remember those who, but for them, would have had a cheerless Christmas....**

-- Chicago Tribune, December 28, 1864

One day in the early spring of 1865, the Civil War finally ended, and with a gradual return to peace and prosperity, more families tried and repeated this visual and increasingly popular form of yuletide celebration called the Christmas tree.

By Christmas of 1879, the Chicago press reflected the country's recovery:

> ...The Christmas tree has now become thoroughly domesticated in this county, and grows as sturdily as in its Teutonic soil, and the little old man of the knapsack and reindeers, who once went the rounds of Scandinavia alone, has travelled over seas and is now familiar with every American chimney. The advent of good times and the more buoyant feeling of our people will unquestionably make his trip a memorable one and load the Christmas trees with rare fruitage....
>
> *-- Chicago Daily Tribune, December 21, 1879*

More "good times" led to increased "domestication" of the Christmas tree:

> ...A day or two ago, 8,000 trees were chopped down and sent in on the [railroad] cars by Santa Claus. He must have nearly three times as many more, because there are nearly 30,000 trees wanted every year in Chicago.... this year, [Santa] is selling them at from 5 cents to $25 apiece. The very large ones are for churches and Sunday-schools, and the very little ones are meant only for the baby.
> Santa Claus has also sent to town great bales of pretty, feathery green sprays of hycopodium, or ground-pine, which grows in large patches in the region of Lake Superior. It is picked by the Indians, packed into bales, and shipped wherever Santa Claus wants it. Ground-pine makes very pretty decoration when its sprays are woven with wire or cord into wreaths and other designs, or into long lines which may be gracefully looped upon the parlor walls. Nobody knows how many thousands of yards of this are sold every winter, but the number must be very large, as it is quite cheap, and costs only 6 to 10 cents per yard....
>
> *-- Chicago Daily Tribune, December 18, 1881*

In the 1880's, Christmas trees were still lighted by means of real wax candles and real flames, with the candles awkwardly atttached to the tree's branches, so the trees, particularly when they began to dry out, posed major fire hazards. Careless people, including impatient children wanting to emulate their parents and light the trees themselves, were often seriously burned and sometimes even killed. In Chicago, several Christmas tree fire casualties involving individuals occurred annually, but once, in the mid-1880's, one blaze had the potential for serious disaster.

On December 25, 1885, the festivities at Chicago's Cook County Hospital featured about 600 people gathered around a gigantic Christmas tree placed in the amphitheater -- at approximately the same spot where anatomical demonstrators from medical colleges trained future doctors by dissecting the bodies of the unclaimed dead in front of a large audience. As "Santa" entered the packed room, the tree suddenly caught on fire from one of its hundreds of candles, and during the three-minute panic that followed, more than 50 people, ranging from County Commissioners and hospital staff to patients, were badly burned and bruised. As one newspaper wrote, "...While the raving multitude was still in an uncontrollable frenzy of fear, screeching women and wailing children were trampled underfoot by the remorseless fugitives...." The amphitheater had only two, small exits -- and the position of the blazing tree and many of the patients' cots rendered one of them useless. Fortunately, no lives were lost, and the hospital became one of the first in the country to invest in the costly new electric Christmas tree lights that had just become available.

Chicago, in the busy 1880's, saw Christmas tree sales increase to the point where vendors had trouble finding places to display all of their coniferous wares. The wooden "sidewalks" in front of stores became the new display areas, seriously impeding pedestrian traffic. One report in December, 1886, described the sidewalk in front of one business as being blocked by "a pile of Christmas trees, thirty feet long, twenty feet high, and occupying nine feet of the street side of the walk."

The 1890's saw increasing sales of Christmas trees in Chicago, giving the final decade of the 19th century a "golden age" glow. Christmas socializing also reached new heights in this decade:

In every hall in all sections of the city where German homes are grouped, there was a ball or entertainment or merrymaking gathering of some sort last night. The same may be said of the districts where Scandinavians abound. There was speech and song, dancing, social converse, and holly....

-- *Chicago Daily Tribune,* December 26, 1890

The Christmas Festival Night of Chicago's Turnverein Vorwaerts (a "Turnverein" was a German "gym" club, and Chicago had several different ones) saw 1,800 people in attendance on December 25, 1891, while the Christmas tree at the city's Germania Club that same night, where "1,500 people thronged the magnificent club building," was 24 feet high with 250 colored electric lights -- red, blue, yellow -- gleaming from its branches, powered by 24 storage batteries lining the wall.

The Chicago Post Office, swamped in an ocean of Christmas parcels, announced, "The Christmas of 1891 has distanced all its predecessors. It is twice as heavy in our line as a year ago."

The press, in late 1892, dubbed Chicago "the busiest city in the world."

Life appeared to be exploding geometrically. The challenge was to keep up with it all.

Shortages of Christmas greenery followed in the first years of the 1900's, with Christmas tree prices jumping, for an average-size tree, from $1.00 to $1.50. Forecasters predicted a resultant drift away from trees ("...Except with Germans and Scandinavians, the Christmas tree is being given up a good deal by Chicagoans...." -- *Chicago Daily Tribune,* December 22, 1904) and towards holly wreaths ("... holly is found in the poorest quarters...." -- same source), with recommendations to give the new "artificial Christmas trees" a try. But the city's continuing prosperity proved the prophets wrong -- for Christmas, 1906, Chicagoans spent a record $300,000 on Christmas trees and greenery decorations alone.

Into those exciting, yet challenging, "Seas of Change" sailed the archaic Christmas Tree Ships, with the old-fashioned Schuenemann brothers navigating many of them.

THREE

Early Christmas Tree Ships

After the Civil War, there developed in the Great Lakes a seasonal opportunity for ambitious freshwater captains to provide an appreciated service for the residents of the rapidly growing cities which developed on the prairie side of Lake Michigan. A few vessels, usually older, maverick schooners which roamed randomly from port to port in quest of cargoes to load and transport, found a windfall opportunity at each year's end to earn a respectable sum of money, sometimes as much as the ship had made during the entire shipping season. For those few vessels, soon to be called the Christmas Tree Ships, the final trip of the year before ice closed the Great Lakes for several months would take them to a northern, wilderness harbor where the crew or hired help would load the ship with freshly cut fir trees. These pine and balsam-scented cargoes were then transported to the prairie ports of Milwaukee and Chicago, there to be sold to annually increasing numbers of urban families struck with the urge to decorate trees inside their homes.

Old, workhorse schooners in the late 1800's and early 1900's were frequently overloaded to get the most out of their transport ability, thereby earning more dollars for their owners who knew that their faltering ships were on their last legs. More often than not, these owners also delayed long-term, preventive maintenance of their obsolete vessels in order to save money, since a replacement ship of slightly better quality could be purchased cheaply and readily. Some people today drive their old cars until the vehicles simply die. Unfortunately, when this attitude, quite common even a century ago, was applied to aging, wooden ships, it was often more than just the vessel that died. Newspapers across the Great Lakes regularly lamented the use of these "floating coffins," particularly late in the shipping season when autumn and winter gales created such severe and dangerous conditions that insurance policies on ships often ended at midnight on the last day of November.

For about 40 years, between the end of the financial crisis of 1873 and the beginning of World War I in 1914, Christmas Tree Ships flourished as a traditional and welcome source of holiday trees for urbanites in prairie ports.

The Christmas Tree Ship yuletide trade appears to have been unique to Lake Michigan, as we have found no references to such activity for any cities on any of the other four Great Lakes. Finding acres of evergreens outside Toronto or Detroit or Cleveland or Buffalo or Duluth apparently was not problematic as it was for Milwaukee and Chicago.

Aging lumber schooners arriving with Christmas trees for their final run of the navigational season, before ice set in and sailors stripped off their vessels' sails and rigging and laid them up in a safe harbor for the duration of the winter, arrived in varying numbers every year from the mid-1870's until 1911. But there was one exception: the year 1880.

The Great Lakes in November of 1880 experienced early cold weather and unusual gales of such ferocity, bitterness, and persistence that it changed the plans for most ship owners. One newspaper in mid-November reported that, "...Our oldest navigators say they never before experienced such cold southwest winds as during the present fall."

The common practice for ship owners was to operate at least until the last day of November -- which, for vessels with good ratings that carried insurance, was usually the day that insurance policies expired. Long before the last day of the month, the press reported, on November 17th, that the schooner *Rouse Simmons* was among the many vessels that, due to the early bad weather showing no signs of letting up, had stripped their sails and rigging and "laid up" for the winter. These early birds were the lucky ones.

Many dozens of other ships still on the lakes were delayed or sunk or damaged by the bad weather. The schooner *Bessie Boalt* was frozen solidly into the ice in White Lake at the edge of Lake Michigan on November 21st, the same day that tugs in the Chicago River could not get above the railroad bridge at the foot of South Water Street because of the thick ice. On Lake Erie, many ships racing to reach winter quarters found themselves frozen in open lake ice, particularly off Toledo and Long Point. The schooner *Ida Keith* was covered with six inches of ice, and her foremast and mizzenmast had been carried away by the bad weather. The tug *Florence* at Cleveland was breaking through the ice and put a hole in her side. On November 23rd, the *Hinckley* was frozen in the ice at Cheboygan at the Straits of Mackinac, where the temperature was 13 degrees below zero. That same day, two schooners, the *Monguagon* and the *Wells Burt,* collided on Lake Michigan in a snowstorm that damaged the rigging of both ships. On November 26th, ice cut a hole into the tug *Samson*, sinking the vessel near Point Pelee in Lake Erie, where ten miles of heavy ice surrounded the Colchester Reef lightship and another 21 ships were frozen solidly in the lake. The schooner *M. E. Tremble* left Buffalo on November 15th, and could not reach Cleveland, 175 miles away, until 13 days later due to the ice. On Lake Huron, Spectacle Reef Lighthouse, completely covered in ice, closed for the season of navigation early, on November 25th, and the schooner *W. Wallace*, with a cargo of salt, sank in Goderich harbor after the ice cut a hole in her hull. On December 2nd, the *Chicago Inter Ocean* reported that "The losses to the insurance companies on cargoes, the past season, are heavier than ever before... There won't be many insurance agents next season...."

It can be understood why no Christmas Tree Ships reached Chicago in the year 1880. Because the Christmas tree cargo was always planned for the final run of the season, the wholly unexpected early closing of navigation due to extreme weather forced many ships to stop operating weeks before their planned "final run."

Maritime historian Fred Neuschel has meticulously researched the careers of many of the ships which carried Christmas trees on Lake Michigan, and we, through our own research, have been able to add some vessels and further information to his impressive list. Here is a chronological listing of them all:

Year	Ship	Ship's Age	Notes
1874	St. Lawrence	32	Schooner, lost a deck load of Christmas trees overboard on Lake Michigan (*Chicago Inter Ocean*, Dec. 20, 1874). Built 1842 at Clayton, NY, 93 feet long, burned 30 miles SE of Milwaukee April 30, 1878, with two lives lost.
1876	Wm. H. Hinsdale	26	This 61-ton schooner took 1,300 Christmas trees to Racine in 1876. It was wrecked in November, 1877, at South Haven, Michigan.
	Reindeer	?	
	Lady Ellen	1	Small, 44-ton schooner built in 1875 at Ahnapee, Wisconsin. Abandoned there ca. 1895.
1877	Lady Ellen	2	See *Chicago Inter Ocean*, Dec. 21, 1877
	Lady Washington	new	Schooner, 76 tons, built in 1877 at Grand Haven, Michigan.
	Alice	?	Sloop, took trees to Milwaukee (*Chicago Inter Ocean*, Dec. 7, 1877)
1878	Dan Newhall	26	Schooner, 100 feet long, built at Milwaukee in 1852, renamed *Ray S. Farr* in 1882, foundered off Michigan City, Ind., Dec. 1, 1886.
1879	Coaster	12	See *Chicago Daily Tribune*, Dec. 14, 1879
	unidentified		"A small schooner arrived in the afternoon with Christmas trees." (*Chicago Daily Tribune*, Dec. 18, 1879)
1880	none	-	-
1881	Coaster	14	Schooner, 85 tons, stranded at Chicago, July 18, 1886.
1882	Iris	16	Two-masted schooner, 62 tons, 74 feet, built at Port Huron, 1866, abandoned at Jackson Harbor, Washington Isl., Wisconsin, 1913.
	Coaster	15	See *Chicago Daily Tribune*, Dec. 8, 1882
1883	Coaster	16	(See above: 1881)
	Robbie Knapp	11	15-ton schooner, built 1872 at Baileys Harbor, Wisconsin, abandoned early 1900's.
	Sea Star	28	91-foot, 95-ton schooner built in 1855 at Irving, NY, wrecked off Ahnapee, Wisconsin, on Nov. 4, 1886.
1884	Sea Star	29	(See above)
1885	Ole Oleson	20	62-ton scow built in 1865 at Oshkosh, Wisconsin, sank in mid-lake Sept. 22, 1887.
	Conquest	32	110-foot, 150-ton schooner built in 1853 at

	Corona	15	Olcott, NY, scuttled off Sheboygan, Wisconsin, in the spring of 1899. 172-foot steamer, built at Manitowoc in 1870. Burned on Nov. 18, 1898, Tonawanda, NY.
1886	*Ole Oleson*	21	(See above: 1885)
	Conquest	33	See *Chicago Daily Tribune*, Dec. 12, 1886
1887	*Supply*	26	August Schuenemann took trees from Ahnapee to Chicago. 89-ton schooner built in 1861 at Black River, Ohio, abandoned in 1895.
	Conquest	34	(See above: 1885)
1888	*Vestey V*	1	95-ton steamer built in 1887 at Grand Haven, Michigan; abandoned in 1895.
1889	*Surprise*	33	120-foot, three-masted, 222-ton schooner built 1856 at Milan, Ohio, abandoned 1900.
	John W. Wright	20	Carried 3,500 trees on this trip. Small 52-foot, 26-ton, two-masted schooner, built at Oshkosh, Wisc., in 1869, abandoned in 1915.
1890	*Industry*	20	73-foot, 55-ton, two-masted schooner, built in 1870 at Manitowoc, Wisconsin, abandoned in 1918.
1891	*Lady Ellen*	16	(See above: 1876)
	John W. Wright	22	(See above: 1889)
1892	*Mary Ludwig*	18	77-ton schooner built at South Haven, Michigan, in 1874. Abandoned at Grand Haven, Michigan, 1918.
	John W. Wright	23	(See above: 1889)
1893	*Thomas C. Wilson*	25	58-foot, 30-ton schooner, built 1868 at Black River, Ohio, stranded and wrecked at Egg Harbor, Wisconsin, Nov., 1902.
1894	*Thomas C. Wilson*	26	See *Chicago Inter Ocean*, Nov. 16, 1894
	Mystic	28	See *Chicago Inter Ocean*, and *(Door County) Advocate*, both dated Nov. 17, 1894
	A. R. Upright	11	See *Chicago Inter Ocean*, Dec. 8, 1894. This small, 24-ton schooner built at Charlevoix, Michigan, in 1883, was abandoned by 1897.
1895	*M. Capron*	20	See *Chicago Daily Tribune*, Oct. 22, 1895
	Seaman	47	See *Sturgeon Bay Advocate*, Oct. 26 and Nov. 3, 1895. This 88-foot, three-masted schooner, built in 1848 at Cleveland, was wrecked on Pilot Island, Lake Michigan, Nov. 15, 1908, with a cargo of potatoes. No lives lost.
	Franc. Miner	10	See *Chicago Daily Tribune,* Nov. 23, 1895. This small, 45-ton schooner was built in 1885 at Green Bay, Wisconsin.
	Augustus	10	See *Chicago Daily Tribune*, Dec. 6, 1895. This small, 71-foot, 45-ton schooner was built in 1885 at Spoonville, Mich., and burned on Nov. 24, 1918, at Red River, Green Bay.

	Mystic	29	Wrecked on Pilot Island, Wisconsin, on Oct. 15, 1895, while on its way to Little Bay de Noc to pick up a cargo of Christmas trees.
1896	*Actor*	6	Small, 21-ton schooner, built at Manitowoc, Wisconsin, in 1890.
	Eugene C. Hart	6	126-foot steamer, built in Manitowoc in 1890, renamed *Norlond* in 1919, sank south of Milwaukee Nov. 13, 1922. It saw very limited use hauling 3,000 trees only once from Rowley's Bay to Sturgeon Bay, where the trees were shipped by train to St. Louis. See *Door County Advocate,* Nov. 28, 1896.
	H. C. Winslow	43	140-foot, 252-ton schooner, built in 1853 at Black R., Ohio, abandoned 1905 at Chicago.
	Kate Hinchman	34	See *Door County Advocate*, Nov. 14, 1896. This 116-foot, 236-ton schooner built in 1862 at Detroit, was abandoned in 1903 near Sturgeon Bay, Wisconsin.
	Margaret Dall	29	112-foot, 176-ton schooner built in 1867 at Michigan City, Indiana, stranded and wrecked at South Manitou Island, Lake Michigan, Dec. 19, 1908.
	Nellie Church	29	123-ton schooner built in 1867 at Fort Howard, Wisconsin.
	Sea Gem	33	103-ton schooner, built at Manitowoc in 1863, sent 8,000 Christmas trees "south" to Chicago; see *The Advocate*, Nov. 28, 1896
	Seaman	48	See *Door County Advocate* and *Chicago Daily Tribune*, Nov. 14, 1896
1897	*Emily and Eliza*	23	78-foot, 63-ton scow schooner built in 1874 at Oak Harbor, Ohio, stranded and wrecked at

There were more than 60 known "Christmas Tree Ships" between 1874 and the early 1900's on Lake Michigan. **Left:** *The schooner,* **Conquest,** *was used in 1885 and 1886.* **Right:** *The* **H.C. Winslow** *carried Christmas trees in 1896.* (KOHL-FORSBERG COLLECTION)

			Aral (near Frankfort), Mich., Sept. 9, 1910.
	Experiment	43	See *Chicago Daily Tribune*, Nov. 13, 1897. 50-ton schooner built in 1854 at St. Joseph, Michigan.
	Kate Hinchman	35	(See above: 1896)
	Little Georgey	27	Sometimes called *Little Gregory,* 52-ton, 81-foot schooner built in 1870 at Sheboygan, Wisconsin, reportedly lost at the Straits of Mackinac in October, 1912.
	Mary L. Collins	43	See *Chicago Daily Tribune*, Nov. 24, 1897. 130-foot, 231-ton schooner, built in 1854 at Toledo, Ohio, used by Capt. Herman Schuenemann in 1897, 1898, 1899, 1900.
	A. J. Mowery		Used by Capt. Herman Schuenemann in the Chicago R. to store Christmas trees, greens.
1898	*Emily and Eliza*	24	(See above: 1897)
	Little Georgey	28	(See above: 1897)
	Mary L. Collins	44	(See above: 1897)
	Monitor	36?	See *Chicago Daily Tribune,* Nov. 25, 1898. This could be the 105-ton schooner, built at Black River, Ohio, in 1862, abandoned in the early 1900's.
	S. Thal	35	Wrecked off Glencoe, Illinois, Nov. 10, 1898, with a cargo of Christmas trees, all hands lost, including Capt. August Schuenemann.
1899	*Mary L. Collins*	45	(See above: 1897)
1900	*Ida*	24	120-foot, 169-ton schooner, built in 1876 at Milwaukee, capsized and sank near Frankfort, Michigan, on Sept. 29, 1908.
	Joses	34	100-foot, 120-ton schooner, built at Holland, Michigan, in 1866, abandoned in 1917.
	Mary L. Collins	46	(See above: 1897)
	Vermont	43	87-foot, 113-ton scow schooner built in 1853 at Huron, Ohio, foundered off Escanaba, Michigan, Sept. 7, 1903.
1901	*Nancy Dell*	22	See *Chicago Daily Tribune*, Dec. 17, 1901. The *Nancy Dell* stranded and broke up, with no lives lost, at South Middle Village, Michigan, on Lake Michigan, on June 21, 1902.
	Georgia	21	195-foot, 895-ton steamer, built as *City of Ludington* 1880 at Manitowoc, Wisc., name changed to *Georgia* in 1898, towed to Big Summer Island 1933 for use as breakwall.
	Caledonia	58	Wrecked off Glen Haven, Mich., with cargo of potatoes, slabs and Christmas trees, Nov. 25, 1901, no lives lost. 70-foot, 52-ton, schooner, built 1843, Southampton, Canada West (Ontario), rebuilt 1861, sold U.S. 1867.

Year	Ship		Description
1902	*Augustus*	17	(See above: 1895)
	O. Shaw	32	Small, 67-foot, 40-ton schooner built in 1870 at South Haven, Michigan, wrecked in a storm off Calumet, Illinois, Aug. 9, 1904.
	Truman Moss	35	See *Chicago Daily Tribune*, Nov. 24, 1902. 130-foot, 219-ton schooner, built in 1867 at Sandusky, Ohio, abandoned in 1911.
1903	*Charly J. Smith*	24	43-ton, 60-foot, two-masted schooner, built in 1879 at South Haven, Michigan, was abandoned at Little Sturgeon Bay, WI, in 1905.
	George L. Wrenn	35	214-ton schooner built in 1868 at Fort Howard, Wisconsin, abandoned in Chicago River 1910-1911.
1904	*George L. Wrenn*	36	Herman Schuenemann, captain in 1904
	Margaret Dall	37	(See above: 1896)
1905	*George L. Wrenn*	37	(See above: 1903)
	Augustus	20	(See above: 1895)
1906	*George L. Wrenn*	38	Herman Schuenemann, captain in 1906
	Larabida	30	59-foot, 39-ton, three-masted schooner, ex-*Jessie Winter*, built 1876 at Sheboygan
	Melitta	25	88-foot, 68-ton schooner, built in 1881 at Manitowoc, Wisconsin, abandoned in 1923.
1907	*George L. Wrenn*	39	(See above: 1903)
1908	*George L. Wrenn*	40	(See above: 1903)
1909	*George L. Wrenn*	41	Herman Schuenemann, captain in 1909
	Bertha Barnes	37	Used by Herman Schueneman in 1909. See *Chicago Inter Ocean*, Dec. 7, 1909. 151-foot, 330-ton, three-masted schooner, built 1872 at Sheboygan, Wisc., renamed *W. D. Hossack* in 1911, sold off-lakes in 1916, foundered off Cuba's Isle of Pines on Aug. 4, 1920.
	Augustus	24	(See above: 1895)

Left: *The schooner,* Joses, *carried Christmas trees on Lake Michigan in 1900.* **Right:** *The* **Truman Moss** *did the same in 1902.* (Kohl-Forsberg Collection)

	Melitta	28	(See above: 1906)
1910	*Rouse Simmons*	42	Herman Schuenemann, captain in 1910
	Watkins	?	tugboat
1911	*Rouse Simmons*	43	Charles Nelson, captain in 1911
1912	*Rouse Simmons*	44	Wrecked off Two Rivers, Wisconsin, Nov. 23, 1912, while returning to Chicago with a cargo of Christmas trees, with all hands lost, including Herman Schuenemann.
	Oneida	53	Used only to sell trees from its deck in 1912 as a dockside substitute for the *Rouse Simmons*. The 138-foot, 201-ton *Oneida*, built in 1857 at Ashtabula, Ohio, was abandoned in 1917, broken up at Sturgeon Bay in the 1920's.
1913	*D'Artagnan*	?	
	J. V. Taylor	46	125-foot, 200-ton schooner, built in 1867 at Winneconne, Wisconsin, abandoned in 1928.
1914	*Arendal*	41	123-foot, 210-ton, three-masted schooner, built 1873 at Sheboygan, WI, abandoned in 1918. Used as dockside Christmas tree ship.
1915	*C. H. Hackley*	47	130' schooner, built 1868, at Milwaukee. Sold off-lakes and scrapped in Florida in 1931.
1917	*Minnie Mueller*	49	126-foot, 199-ton, three-masted schooner, built 1868 at Fort Howard, Wisconsin, already lay abandoned in the Chicago River when it was used as a Christmas tree ship in 1917 at dockside only.
1919	*Wisconsin*	?	gasoline-powered vessel
	Liberty	?	Carried 100,000 spruces to Chicago
1920	*Beaver*	?	tugboat
1922	*Lillian*	?	gasoline-powered vessel
	White Swan	18	diesel-powered vessel

Date(s) unknown: the schooner *Mary E. Packard* (96-foot, 101-ton, two-masted scow schooner built at South Haven, 1875, abandoned in 1908) also hauled Christmas trees.

When the schooner *Conquest* arrived in Chicago with a cargo of Christmas trees in 1886, one newspaper reported in detail:

......the schooner, *Conquest*,...lies in the river with something like 6,000 spruce and balsam Christmas-trees. The trees were cut about two weeks ago near Ahnapee, Wis., and vary in size from three to twenty-five feet in length. Those between three and twelve feet in length are termed "house trees," and are worth in wholesale from $12 to $15 per hundred. Those between fourteen and twenty-five feet come under the appellation of "church and hall trees" and are worth from $1.50 to $15 each. The Captain said yesterday that the orders were just beginning to come in, as the season was hardly under way. He thought he should have no difficulty whatever in selling every tree he had. There were only two other vessels in the river with similar cargoes, and they were small ones. The supply by vessel this year was not more than half as large at this time last year, though prices were about the same.

-- *Chicago Daily Tribune*, December 12, 1886

The Chicago River was, in the late 1800's, becoming a massive garbage dump for old, wooden ships when their owners reached the point where they no longer trusted the vessels' integrity and feared to take them out on the open lake. But they were impediments to navigation in the narrow branches of the Chicago River. In 1898, the *Chicago Daily Tribune* made an appeal for "House-Cleaning:"

> **What becomes of the old wooden sailing-vessels -- the white-winged fleet of barks, brigs, and schooners -- when they have grown old?**
>
> **The day is near at hand when any one who wishes can see the question answered, for the Chicago River is soon to receive its infrequent "house cleaning." Last week Captain John Roberts, harbormaster, made a trip up the river to see for himself the craft which have no more part in the busy life of the lakes and to select those fit to be taken out into deep water and sunk....**
>
> **A block north... lies the old *A. J. Mowry* [sic; should be *A. J. Mowery*], known to all the veteran sailors and masters of the lakes. The *Mowry* was built in 1863 at Milan, O., and at one time was fitted out as a steam barge. Its bottom at the present time, however, would not stand the weight of a steam engine, as its posts and ribs are so soft with rot that the fingers can dig holes clear through the biggest of them. A moderate sized sea on the lake would shake it up so, says an old friend of the boat, that it would begin to disintegrate, and would go to pieces.... Even lying quietly at the dock, with the hawser running across the deck and around the mast stump, for a plank cannot be found in the old *Mowry* which would hold a staple tightly, it finds it difficult to keep afloat. It was used last winter to store Christmas trees in, and its hold at the present time contains many of the trees and bales of green wreaths that were not sold. It is probable that the old *Mowry* will suffer the fate in store for all old-timers, and that it will be towed out into the lake to be sunk....**

But the vast size of Chicago's growing population, with increasing numbers of Christmas tree advocates, should make it logical that a few old schooners could not satisfy the city's enormous market demands. Trains had been supplying Chicago's grocers and market place sellers with Christmas trees for decades. In 1902, for example, it was reported that an average of 150 train carloads, each containing 2,000 trees, arrived annually in the city. "Some of [the trees] are brought in by vessels, but not many," continued the same report in the *Chicago Daily Tribune* on December 7, 1902. Trains easily conveyed to Chicago 85% to 95% of the Christmas trees purchased annually, while ships brought the remainder.

The Christmas Tree Ships coming to Chicago served three purposes. First, they offered sentimental elements of nostalgia, particularly after about 1895 when schooners, gradually fading from commercial usage, became increasingly rare sights to the average person. Second, the schooners offered dramatic venues that were fun by giving fathers, mothers and children a chance to walk around on a vintage sailing ship in the Chicago River to buy a Christmas tree -- compared to the common and too familiar setting of the local grocer's store or a city market place. Third, with hard work and some luck, a schooner owner could make a windfall profit from this final trip with Christmas trees, sometimes as much money as his ship made for him the entire rest of the year hauling lumber. It would be quite unrealistic to think that the Christmas Tree Ships, by themselves, satisfied Chicago's enormous appetite for trees.

Often the lumber schooner's final run of the season with a cargo of Christmas trees was a challenging experience, obviously very dependent upon the weather at the most dangerous time of the year. This was reported in late 1903:

> **Despite the series of storms which during the last two weeks has driven Lake Michigan's schooner fleet into winter quarters, Chicago is not to be deprived of Christmas greens. Early to-day, the schooner *George L. Wrenn* reached port after a remarkably fast run from the foot of Lake Michigan, bringing several thousand Christmas trees and tons upon tons of green boughs for decorative purposes.**
>
> **The *Wrenn* is the first of the Christmas tree fleet this year, and to South Manistique, Mich., belongs the credit of sending forward her cargo. The schooner suffered from heavy seas on her trip, and after being docked at the foot of Clark street sailors spent several hours removing a coating of ice from her sides and deck.**
>
> *-- Chicago Evening Post,* November 21, 1903

The 58-year-old schooner, *Caledonia*, and its three crewmembers, had been less fortunate in November, 1901. The headlines screamed drama: "Almost Dead From Exposure," "Members of Crew of Schooner *Caledonia* Wrecked Monday," "Men Were Badly Frozen, But Were Finally Resuscitated," "Three Kenosha Men Nearly Perish After Wreck of Their Schooner," "Rescued from Their Yawl After Night's Battle with the Waves." The ship had left Boyne City, Michigan, on Sunday night, November 24th, with 600 bushels of potatoes below deck, and Christmas trees and slabs piled on deck. The ship leaked, the men pumped, but worsening conditions forced them to abandon the schooner in their small yawl boat at 5 AM on November 25th, when they were off Glen Haven, Michigan. The *Caledonia* then, in the darkness, capsized and presumably sank. The three men spent 27 hours adrift before the schooner *Lomie A. Burton* rescued the bitterly cold, suffering sailors, their wet clothing frozen to the yawl's planking, and took them to their destination, Milwaukee -- but minus their ship and their Christmas trees.

Of the many ships that labored in the business of providing families with Christmas trees during those years, one vessel is unique. Perhaps because of its affable, hardworking commander who personalized the work he did for his faithful clients, or maybe due to the ship's tragic demise in the fury of a fierce storm just prior to the festive holiday season, ironically while it sailed en route to providing yuletide joy to children and adults alike, the story of this Christmas Tree Ship has grown into unforgettable and legendary proportions with its annual retellings and dramatizations.

That commander was Captain Herman Schuenemann of Chicago, and his Christmas Tree Ship was named the *Rouse Simmons*.

Above: *The three-masted Great Lakes schooner,* **Rouse Simmons** *-- the famous "Christmas Tree Ship" of the early 20th century.* (Kohl-Forsberg Collection)

Below: *This 19th-century painting alleges to be German religious reformer Martin Luther's family enjoying a candle-lit tree at Christmas, 1536.* (Kohl-Forsberg Collection)

Left: *In the first half of the 1800's, before Christmas trees became universally popular in private homes, a variety of greens -- fir boughs, myrtle, holly, along with red berries -- were cut and used extensively to decorate residences, providing us with the predominant colors of Christmas still with us today, namely bright red and rich green. This cover artwork for sheet music to "The Jovial Christmas Polka" depicts not only a lavishly ornamented, upper-class dining room, but also the liberal use of presumably alcoholic beverages to help make the occasion "jovial."* (KOHL-FORSBERG COLLECTION)

Right: *In Great Britain, Queen Victoria and her husband, Prince Albert, famously set up a Christmas tree, decorated with candy, cookies, sweetmeats, gingerbread, glacé fruits, and small gifts, and illuminated by candles, for their children in their royal household at Windsor Castle in 1848. The royal family established an annual tradition quickly copied by many of the queen's middle-class subjects when they saw this full-page drawing in* **The Illustrated London News** *that year. Prince Albert was from the German province of Saxe-Coburg, and Queen Victoria considered the Christmas tree tradition, which had already existed sporadically among a few members of the royal family in England, worthy of grand-scale emulation.* (KOHL-FORSBERG COLLECTION)

Right: *Early artists in the United States, aware of the Nordic connection to both the Christmas Tree and to Santa Claus, drew him wearing northern European garb, with a short-skirted tunic edged with fur, muscular legs clearly displayed above knee-length boots, an image more representative of a Scandinavian god such as Woden or Thor than anything pertaining to Christianity. This is the cover of the weekly news tabloid* **Harper's Weekly** *from January 2, 1869. Early detractors of the Christmas tree in the USA, the Puritans and others, pointed to the ancient Scandinavian-Germanic heathen worship of oak trees as reason enough not to place any kind of a tree inside a Christian home in celebration of Christmas.*
(KOHL-FORSBERG COLLECTION)

Left: *The special Christmas drawings by German-born (from the town of Landau in the Rhineland-Palatinate) American artist Thomas Nast (1840-1902), published mainly in* **Harper's Weekly** *near the end of every year between 1863 and 1887, established the rotund, jovial, greenery-bedecked image of Santa Claus for generations of children in the Victorian era and beyond. Thomas Nast is credited with giving us the widely recognized version of Santa Claus we have today, and yellowing newspapers containing his Christmas artwork are highly sought by collectors.*
(KOHL-FORSBERG COLLECTION)

By the early 1900's, the powerful, god-like evergreen tree (it stayed green all winter!) was firmly established as a Christmas symbol, and was frequently used on the suddenly ubiquitous Christmas card, most often printed in Germany. (KOHL-FORSBERG COLLECTION)

The Christmas Tree steps -- from cutting, to marketplace selling, to decorating, and, finally, un-decorating -- appeared on 1890's French cards. (Kohl-Forsberg Collection)

Above: *By the late 1800's, increasing numbers of people worked in the growing Christmas tree industry. This seasonal business had a very small window of opportunity, and trees had to reach public markets as fast as possible.* (KOHL-FORSBERG COLLECTION)

Below: *Christmas trees were first sold at public market places, soon replaced by lots used exclusively for selling trees. This* **Harper's Weekly** *appeared only a few weeks after the tragic loss of the Christmas Tree Ship in 1912.* (KOHL-FORSBERG COLLECTION)

FATHER CHRISTMAS—"UP-TO-DATE."

Wishing You the best of Christmas Joys

Above: *England's* Punch *magazine showed a very modern Santa hauling Christmas trees in an automobile in 1896! An American Christmas card from 1906 depicted a scene very few people in the real world could afford to replicate: driving around in the countryside in an automobile to cut one's own tree.* (KOHL-FORSBERG COLLECTION)

Below: *Ships, in reality rarely used to transport Christmas trees, nonetheless appeared on Christmas cards, complete with a lighted Christmas tree at the bow, to welcome in the New Year.* (KOHL-FORSBERG COLLECTION)

With best wishes for a happy New Year

Above: *Sailors and Christmas trees: "Christmas Morning -- At the Mast-head" in England's* **The Graphic,** *Christmas, 1879. "Christmas Greetings" (to a lightship crew), cover of* **Harper's Weekly,** *December 28, 1889.* (KOHL-FORSBERG COLLECTION)

Below: Harper's Weekly *published a two-page centerspread called "The Christmas Tree Ship" in the early 1900's (no date on pages).* (KOHL-FORSBERG COLLECTION)

THE CHRISTMAS-TREE SHIP

The December 25, 1880, issue of **Harper's Week-**
ly *featured Christmas Tree business. As the paper
wrote, "On our first page will be found an illustra-
tion of the manner in which the Christmas trees
and wreaths so abundant in our markets in the
holiday season are gathered and prepared....the
business of weaving them is intrusted* [sic] *chiefly
to women and children, who become very expert
at the task. The trade in these wreaths and trees is
quite extensive, and gives employment to a large
number of people." The Schuenemann women
and family friends made wreaths in the Chicago
River on board the ship that brought the trees from
the north woods.* (Kohl-Forsberg Collection)

Various schooners were used to sell Christmas trees from the Chicago River. **Above,** *the* **George L. Wrenn** *and* **John Mee***; at left, the* **Arendall;** *below, unidentified.* (Kohl-Forsberg Collection)

Above: *In 1895, Capt. Herman Schuenemann chartered the 112-foot-long scow schooner* Mystic *to bring trees to Chicago, but the ship was wrecked on Pilot Island in Death's Door before it could pick up its cargo.* (DOOR COUNTY HISTORICAL MUSEUM)

Below: *The schooner* Melitta, *temporarily stranded in this postcard, carried Christmas trees in 1906 and 1909. The 88-foot-long schooner, built at Manitowoc in 1881, was abandoned, reportedly at Detroit, Michigan, in 1923.* (KOHL-FORSBERG COLLECTION)

Above: *Although many different schooners were used to bring Christmas trees to Chicago in the late 1800's and early 1900's, the* **Rouse Simmons** *became the most famous of them all, despite being docked at the Clark Street bridge selling trees from her decks only in two years: 1910 and 1911. The year 1912 proved tragic for the vessel and crew.* (ART COURTESY OF AND © ERIC FORSBERG. SEE WWW.FORSBERGART.COM)

Below: *In the* **Rouse Simmons'** *44-year history, she had several close calls in dangerous situations. One of her most precarious experiences occurred on May 21, 1891, when she left Chicago with the schooner* **Thomas Hume,** *both ships light and bound for Muskegon to pick up lumber cargoes. A violent storm developed in mid-lake, so intense that the* **Rouse Simmons** *turned back to Chicago. The* **Thomas Hume** *(below, right), pressing on, went missing without a trace with all seven hands. The* **Thomas Hume** *was located in 150 feet of water about 24 miles northeast of Chicago in 2003 by* **A & T Recovery.** (ART COURTESY OF AND © ERIC FORSBERG. SEE WWW.FORSBERGART.COM)

Above: *The 44-year-old lumber schooner,* **Rouse Simmons,** *battled a severe storm on Lake Michigan on November 22-23, 1912, while attempting to sail from Thompson, near Manistique, Michigan, south to Chicago with a very heavy cargo of Christmas trees. An unknown number of men was on board, including a few lumberjacks (hired to cut the Christmas trees) hitching a ride to Chicago. Estimates range from 14 to 18 men in all. Besides feeling responsible for the crew's and passengers' lives, Herman Schuenemann had to financially salvage his 1912 season by quickly reaching Chicago and selling his trees.* (ART COURTESY OF AND © ERIC FORSBERG. SEE WWW.FORSBERGART.COM)

Below: *The Rouse Simmons was last seen desperately flying a distress flag several miles off shore in the Kewaunee-Two Rivers area of Wisconsin.* (MAP BY CRIS KOHL)

Above: *The* **Rouse Simmons** *on Sturgeon Bay.*   (Door County Historical Museum)
Below: *Capt. Herman Schuenemann* (center) *stood in 1909 surrounded by trees on the*
   George L. Wrenn, one of the Christmas Tree Ships, in Chicago with two of his crew,
   W. L. Vanaman (left) *and a sailor named Colberg.*   (Kohl-Forsberg Collection)

Right: *Capt. Schuenemann's oldest daughter, Elsie, helped lead the family's annual efforts after their 1912 losses to retain the Christmas Tree Ship custom in Chicago. This photo of her when she was 23 appeared in the* **Chicago Daily News,** *December 6, 1915.*
(KOHL-FORSBERG COLLECTION)

Below: *Elsie's younger sisters, twins Hazel and Pearl, at age 19 in a 1917 photo in the* **Chicago Daily News.** *They were only 14 when the* **Simmons** *sank.*
(KOHL-FORSBERG COLLECTION)

Above: *A year after the tragic loss of the* **Rouse Simmons,** *an axe-wielding widow Barbara Schuenemann directed the cutting and loading of thousands of Christmas trees so she could keep up her family's tradition of selling them from the deck of an old schooner near the Clark Street bridge on the Chicago River. These photos appeared in the* **Chicago Daily Tribune** *on December 13, 1913.*   (KOHL-FORSBERG COLLECTION)

Below: *Barbara Schuenemann maintained the tradition until her death 21 years after her husband died on the* **Rouse Simmons.** *His body was never found, but his name and date of death appear on the headstone in Chicago's Acacia Cemetery, alongside Barbara's name, sharing the silhouette of a single Christmas tree.* (PHOTO BY CRIS KOHL)

FOUR

The Schuenemanns

Herman Schuenemann was born in the Lake Michigan harbor town of Ahnapee (renamed Algoma in 1897), Wisconsin, to German parents in 1865. By the time he was in his early 20's, he had partnered with August, the brother who was 12 years Herman's senior, in the Great Lakes shipping business.

August Schuenemann had become a lake captain already in 1877, hauling lumber cargoes in the holds and upon the decks of older schooners which he could purchase for a few hundred dollars each. In late 1876, August may have been working as a sailor on board the small schooner, *William H. Hinsdale,* when it carried Christmas trees to Racine. The following year, in October, 1877, he became master (captain) of the *Hinsdale,* only to see it wrecked two weeks later when it was driven into the pier at South Haven, Michigan. He and his two crewmembers survived his first shipwreck.

In the summer of 1880, August Schuenemann was given command of the 25-year-old schooner, *Sea Star,* but he was not the captain when that ship was wrecked off Ahnapee on November 4, 1886. In the summer of 1886, August worked as captain of the 21-year-old schooner, *Ole Oleson,* but he was no longer its master when that ship sank in a storm in the middle of Lake Michigan in September, 1887.

For August Schuenemann, life was simply a matter of staying one step ahead of the next shipwreck.

August definitely carried his first cargo of Christmas trees by the mid-1880's. Newspaper accounts often named the Christmas Tree Ships, but not always the captains, during these late-season runs, so it is unclear precisely when August Schuenemann started in that particular sideline of work. He did, however, meet with such success that similar year's end runs became routine for him, and, later, for his younger brother, Herman.

In May, 1889, the Schuenemann brothers invested $1,400 by purchasing a 37-year-old, 95-foot-long schooner named the *Josephine Dresden,* a graceful ship with slender, curved lines that made it stand apart from the many box-like scow schooners on the lakes. They used this ship extensively for several years in the Lake Michigan lumber trade, with Herman working as the manager, and August as the vessel's captain, reflecting the former's ability to deal with people and arrange business deals, and the latter's "hands-on" operation and maintenance of the actual ship.

August had lived in Chicago temporarily during winters when nautical work ceased on the frozen waters of Lake Michigan. For example, in early 1881, he worked as a streetcar operator before returning to his lumber schooner that spring. August moved to Chicago full-time when he married Rose Whiteneck there in 1884. A daughter, Elma, was born in 1885, and a son, Arthur, followed in 1891. Herman, too, lived in the Windy City for brief intervals in the 1880's. The ambitious brothers felt the need to escape their agrarian, homestead upbringing and family poverty at Ahnapee, Wisconsin, and the excitement and opportunities of bustling Chicago attracted them like a magnet. They tingled at the thought of reaping the benefits of the city's prosperity.

Although born into a poor and humble family, Herman Schuenemann never failed to look impressively dapper at formal functions. (CHICAGO MARITIME SOCIETY)

The Germans in Chicago numbered about 10% of the population in 1900 -- 200,000 people out of two million. The next largest immigrant group, the Irish, had 100,000 people, or 5% of the city's population. German immigrants had settled mainly in Chicago's near north, and soon, in their community, they had German churches, grocery stores, butcher shops, bakeries, beer gardens and halls, music and singing societies, "turnvereinen" (sports clubs), German newspapers, and, in season of course, Christmas trees and greens, with all of their attendant decorations, cookies, and sweets. The Schuenemanns supplied large Christmas trees annually for most of the local institutions, such as churches, and social organizations like the Germania Club, which was only a block from their home. German was spoken throughout the community, and the Schuenemann brothers held an advantage by being fluent in both English, the language of the country where they were born, and in German, the language their parents used during their upbringing at home in Ahnapee.

The death of their father in Ahnapee in 1889 provided the psychological "cut" needed to catapult them to the big city. Ahnapee, however, remained in the brothers' lives as a business location, and they frequently sailed their ships to and from that harbor where they, fascinated as children, had watched the arrivals, the workings, and the departures of the many "white-winged" schooners and wooden steamships that helped build this community during the golden era of Great Lakes' maritime history.

Herman followed his older brother, August's, footsteps by moving permanently to Chicago in 1889, where he married Barbara Schindel on April 9, 1891. Reflecting the well-known Germanic zeal for precision, exactly nine months to the day after their wedding night, on January 9, 1892, daughter Elsa Christine Louise was born.

August and Herman's mother also made the move from Ahnapee to Chicago in 1892, presumably to be closer to her children and grandchildren.

Sailors worldwide are known as a transient population, an indeterminable number of wanderlusting individuals who are not inclined to grow roots or aspire to "settled" middle class comforts and respectability. So, too, was the situation in the Great Lakes in the latter half of the 19th century and the beginning of the 20th. The Schuenemann brothers, by marrying and establishing household roots in Chicago, tried hard to rise above their humble beginnings in Ahnapee and, later, above the "drifting sailor" stereotype, to establish themselves comfortably in that era's urban middle class, enjoying its modest affluence.

At this time, when sailing ships were being edged out of Great Lakes commerce by large, steel steamers, the brothers Schuenemann could afford to purchase inexpensive, old, wood schooners, utilize them extensively in the shipping trade for a year or two, then replace them with other affordable ships of similar advanced vintage. Often in the mid-1890's

Chicago Inter-Ocean, *Nov. 30, 1910.*
(Kᴏʜʟ-Fᴏʀsʙᴇʀɢ Cᴏʟʟᴇᴄᴛɪᴏɴ)

and operating on shoestring budgets, each of the brothers commanded a ship which would, for its final run of the season, convey a large load of Christmas trees and boughs for wreaths to eager Chicagoans. This final run often pushed the brothers just barely into profitability for the year. Their wives stood beside them as their solid and active business partners.

Herman tended towards the business aspects that allowed him to spend more time at home with his wife and daughter, while August's inclinations leaned more towards facing the weather and the waves, and actually maintaining and sailing their ships. The brothers and their wives made a good business team.

August Schuenemann first mastered a ship carrying Christmas trees, which was the scow, *Sea Star*, in 1883. This was followed by Christmas tree cargoes in the schooner, *Ole Oleson*, in 1886, and the scow *Supply* in 1887.

In 1893, they sold the schooner *Josephine Dresden* that they had operated for four years. In late 1893, the brothers chartered the schooner, *Thomas C. Wilson*, and used it to haul Christmas trees to Chicago. Impressed with the *Wilson*, they purchased the schooner for $900 in October, 1894, placing that ship's ownership in Rose Schuenemann's name, August's wife -- presumably so as not to have their ship seized by authorities if they were ever libeled and sued. The *Door County Advocate* of November 17, 1894, reported that "...The schooner *J. C. Wilson* [sic], Capt. Schuenemann, cleared for Chicago the first of the week with a cargo of Christmas trees." Eight months later, in June, 1895, they sold the *Wilson* for $600. It appears that the brothers had bought the old schooner mainly, perhaps even exclusively, to haul Christmas trees in late 1894.

In 1894, Herman, always one to consider new opportunities, partnered in a

The **Josephine Dresden,** *low in the water with a heavy load of lumber at Sheboygan, was owned by the Schuenemann brothers from 1889 to 1893.* (KOHL-FORSBERG COLLECTION)

grocery business, but it did not work out.

In late 1895, both brothers worked hard at the Christmas tree branch of their maritime interests. August Schuenemann was in Sturgeon Bay, Wisconsin, preparing their newly-purchased 47-year-old schooner, *Seaman,* for the holiday trade -- the *Door County Advocate* of October 26th wrote, "...Capt. A. L. Schuenemann reports that he has upward of a thousand Christmas trees cut and ready to load so far, and more are being gotten out daily," updated on Saturday, Nov. 23rd, with

> **The schooner *Seaman*, Capt. A. L. Schuenemann, which has been in port after a cargo of Christmas trees for the Chicago market for the past two months, got away along about midnight Sunday.... The *Seaman* had on in the neighborhood of 8,000 trees and 600 bundles of brush....**

Simultaneously, younger brother Herman chartered the schooner, *Mystic*, which had been in competition with them when it carried trees to Chicago in 1894. The *Mystic*, however, met her end by stranding and becoming a total wreck on Pilot Island on October 15, 1895, while on its way north to pick up Herman's trees. Undaunted, he quickly chartered another ship, as reported on November 2, 1895, in the *Door County Advocate*:

> **The deck staysail schooner *M. Capron* is in port after a cargo of Christmas trees for Chicago, having been chartered by Capt. H. Schuenemann for the trip. The *Capron* was to have gone after the outfit of the schooner *Mystic*, ashore on Pilot Island, but owing to the smoky atmosphere the first of the week, the steamer *M & M* was sent for it. At the time the *Mystic* went ashore she was on her way to Little Bay de Noquette [sic] for a load of Christmas trees for Capt. Schuenemann, who had hired the vessel for that purpose.**

Captain Herman Schuenemann, at left, takes a break with his Christmas Tree Ship crew, circa 1909, to pose for a photograph. Because the trees are on display (as opposed to packed for shipping), the location is likely the Chicago River. The vessel could be the schooner, **Bertha Barnes.**
(CHICAGO MARITIME SOCIETY)

The flexible Herman Schuenemann, blessed with an open mind for business diversification (or perhaps running out of time to fill the *M. Capron* completely with trees), "...will not load a full cargo of Christmas trees, but will probably complete the load with potatoes." (*Door County Advocate,* November 9, 1895.)

Both brothers, despite obstacles, managed to get Christmas Tree Ships to Chicago in late 1895, as did some of their competitors.

In between their many Christmas seasons, the brothers were kept busy operating lumber schooners during the spring and summer months.

In 1896, August captained the schooner, *Seaman*, when it carried Christmas trees to Chicago. In late 1897, he chartered, as well as captained, the 43-year-old schooner, *Experiment,* to transport trees, while Herman had purchased another 43-year-old schooner, the *Mary L. Collins*, to bring in more trees for them that year. Herman also made arrangements to store the extra trees in the old hulk of the schooner *A. J. Mowery* in the Chicago River, and to sell them from there.

On December 19, 1897, the *Chicago Daily Tribune* printed a promotional article called "Cut The Yule Trees," with the subheading "Men Who Make It a Business to Supply Chicago":

> A veritable section of northern Michigan -- a forest of 100,000 trees -- lies moored at the south end of Clark street bridge, and disputes with the river the right to make the neighborhood odorous. It is the contribution of the wilderness to Christmas festivities....
>
> The wilds of Wisconsin have been scoured for decades till, in the parlance of those who supply the market, "they are cleaned out to trimmings." For a time, of course, there was an apparently unexhaustible [sic] supply, but the prodigality of Christmas celebrants has of late made it more and more difficult to meet the demand ....
>
> The supply this year is said to be considerably smaller than in former years,.... Few, it is expected, will come into the city by sail, owing to the virtual abandonment of the Wisconsin fields. The business is centralized in fewer hands and boatmen get the benefit of the transportation.
>
> "This is the hardest year Christmas tree men have ever had," said H. Schuneman [sic] of the schooner *A. J. Mowery.* "All our trees came from the 'Soo' and we went inland twenty miles or more to get them. Others had about the same experience. It will not be long before the territory adjacent to the lake in Michigan will be as denuded of Christmas tree stuff as Wisconsin is, and going back into the wilds is attended with difficulties.
>
> "You see, we have to keep near the line of some railroad, and we can't go too far back from the line because it is a big job to drag thousands of trees through the thickets.... What's more, there isn't a fortune in the business nowadays.... the labor involved in cutting and hauling [the trees] in the woods and the transportation charges eat up the profits.
>
> "People have odd notions about Christmas trees. They seem to think that they are largely the tips of trees used in the lumber business -- in short, the refuse of an industry. As a matter of fact, every Christmas tree offered for sale in Chicago is an entire tree in itself, and is specially sought. Many of the thickets where we have to get them are so dense one can scarcely force his way through, and growing in such a condition the trees are apt to be one-sided or otherwise misshapen. A bushman will often have to examine a

hundred or two trees before he gets one that is perfect enough in shape to be of use. One has to go through a big territory to get an ordinary schooner load...."

Free publicity like this was always welcomed. Life was good for the Schuenemann brothers at Christmas, 1897. But it was their last Christmas together.

*   *   *   *   *   *   *   *   *

A roaring northeast wind swept across Lake Michigan for 36 unrelenting hours, attempting to destroy anything made by the hands of man that dared to risk a presence on those open waters.

Desperately trying to remain afloat, a small schooner battled the elements only a few hundred feet off the rocky beach and high shoreline at Glencoe, Illinois, just north of Chicago.

People safely on land, bearing telescopes, binoculars and opera glasses, watched this struggle periodically throughout the afternoon on Wednesday, November 9th, 1898. John Casey, working on the noisy, wave-battered beach, saw that the ship had dropped an anchor and flew its flag at half-mast, indicating a distress signal. Despite the intermittent mist and light fog, he claimed he saw five men working on the deck, including at the helm and manning the pumps, and that they appeared successful in their efforts to keep the ship afloat.

Arthur Lind, an engineer at the Winnetka pumping station, finished his lunch when he looked out and saw the laboring schooner. He reached for his spy glass and climbed to the top of the water tower to get a better view. A larger, three-masted schooner further offshore skipped along in the fierce winds, just barely able to combat nature's efforts to drive it into shore, but the smaller ship, already forced close to the rocky edge and bobbing precariously in boulder-strewn waters, clearly struggled. In mid-afternoon, Lind witnessed the helmsman, who was apparently the vessel's captain, lose his hat in the strong wind, and he remained bareheaded, apparently having no replacement.

Lind watched as the crew, at one point, prepared to get underway again. With sails set and anchor weighed, the vessel moved forward quickly, but a sudden, powerful gust of wind tore its foresail to shreds. Sails came down and the anchor was dropped again. Then fog rolled in and Lind lost visual contact.

The next morning, Thursday, November 10th, Lind gazed across the horizon and, not seeing the ship, breathed a sigh of relief at the probability that they had been able to ride out the fierce winds before successfully resuming their voyage. But his spy glass told a very different story. It showed him planking floating along the shoreline for at least a mile. He sounded a general alarm.

Searchers on the shoreline found empty trunks of the type frequently used by sailors, strips of planking which had once been sections of the deck, splintered parts of ship's masts, and a battered 14-foot-long yawlboat. A mile from the foot of Glencoe's central street, the entire stern of the unfortunate schooner had washed ashore in a little cove, the vessel's name clearly visible on the transom: *S. Thal*.

August Schuenemann commanded the 31-year-old, worn-out schooner, *S. Thal,* for which he had just paid the low price of $250, absurdly inexpensive even by 1898 valuations, but he had also just paid the price for his daring and his frugality -- with his life.

The 55-gross-ton schooner *S. Thal,* built in 1867 at Oshkosh, Wisconsin, measured 75 feet in length and carried two masts. A surprisingly fast ship in her early years, the *Thal* experienced situations considered common, e.g. in early October, 1885, the vessel, after springing a leak during a storm, was purposely beached about ten miles west of Michigan City, Indiana, in order to save the lives of her crew. A tugboat pulled the slightly damaged *Thal* off the beach within a few days.

The *S. Thal* had, in earlier years, been a solid, little moneymaker:

> **The flat-bottom schooner S. Thal is one of the most profitable craft for her inches on the lakes. Although carrying upward of 50,000 feet of lumber, it takes only three men to run her, and this leaves a pretty good margin for the owners, one of whom is the master, Capt. Wm. Robinson. The *Thal* was built on Lake Winnebago and brought to these waters a few years afterward. He has been running between this port** [Sturgeon Bay, Wisconsin] **and Milwaukee nearly all the past fall.**
>
> *-- Door County Advocate,* November 30, 1889

August Schuenemann became the owner of the *S. Thal* through financial misfortune. A young man named Otto Parker (described later in a court document as "an emancipated minor 19 years old") had signed on as cook on board the *S. Thal* in Milwaukee on April 20th, 1898, at a salary of $25 a month. On August 20th, he

No photographs have surfaced of the 55-ton, 75-foot-long S. Thal, *built in 1867, but the* Glen Cuyler, *a two-masted, 49-ton schooner with a length of 72.5 feet, was very similar. The* Cuyler, *built in 1859, was abandoned in 1918.* (Kohl-Forsberg Collection)

quit the services of that vessel, demanding the $100.00 in wages owed to him for his four months of service. Owner William Robertson paid him only $34, so Parker libeled the schooner for the $66 still owed. Robertson did not have the money to pay Parker, so the *S. Thal* was sold to satisfy the claim against it.

The old ship changed hands more than once over the next month, and by late September, 1898, August sailed her from Milwaukee to Sturgeon Bay:

> **Captain A. L. Schuenemann is in port with the small schooner *S. Thal*, which he recently purchased from Milwaukee parties. Captain Schuenemann will load her with Christmas trees for the Chicago market. The *Thal* was recently sold at marshall sale at Milwaukee for $70. It is understood that Captain Schuenemann put up $200 [sic; it was $250] for her at a private sale. The vessel is now undergoing a hauling over, and after receiving some new rigging and painting, she will receive cargo.**

> *-- Door County Advocate,* October 1, 1898

Particularly short of funds at this point, August, like Herman, was quick to make a deal to keep his business plans on course, ultimately a tragic course:

> **...While here Captain [August] Schuenemann of the *Thal*, did not have sufficient funds with which to purchase a Christmas tree cargo, the amount lacking being $100. Captain Schuenemann induced Mr. Hay to sign a note with him at one of the local banks for the amount, giving him as security the ownership of the schooner *S. Thal*, the vessel's marine papers having been made out to that effect. The note was for 90 days, but as the vessel and crew have been lost the estate will be minus the amount. Capt. Schuenemann paid $250 for the vessel at Milwaukee about two months ago. In addition to this claim it is understood that a local groceryman has a bill of $50 against the craft for supplies, and this will also prove a loss.**

> *-- Door County Advocate,* November 26, 1898

Capt. August Schuenemann sailed the *S. Thal*, loaded with 3,500 trees and 540 bundles of brush, out of Sturgeon Bay harbor on Sunday, November 6, 1898, the same day that the *Josephine Dresden,* a finer, larger ship that August had owned a mere five years earlier, also departed. It is possible that August felt some misgivings about having sold that vessel, and also about he ship he now commanded.

Newspapers condemned the schooner *S. Thal* with words like "a tramp" and "decrepit, old vessel," and clearly indicated that the ship was too old to depart from any port. Accounts varied as to the number of people on board the *Thal*, ranging from three to six. The *Door County Advocate*, on January 7, 1899, boldly stated, "...Crew of three lost, not five, as has always been reported." It is completely logical that the cash-strapped August Schuenemann would have kept the paid crew down to the absolute minimum, two people, and that his own salary would come later when the Christmas trees were sold. Only two sailors, besides the captain, were named in news accounts: Turner Davis, who, with his wife, boarded at the August Schuenemann residence in Chicago, and who had been pursuaded by August to work as the ship's mate, and a sailor known only as "Old John."

Surprisingly, none of the bodies from the *S. Thal* was recovered. One newspaper account suggested that the bodies could be tangled in the ship's rigging, particularly if the sailors had tied themselves to a mast before the ship sank. Another theorized that, during the night, the sailors had managed to extract the ship from its anchorage close to shore, but the vessel sank in deeper water just out from "Stone Haven," the impressive residence of Melville E. Stone, off which they had anchored earlier, and that the bodies remained with the shipwreck in deeper water.

Imagine the terror in two boys named Sidney Morris and William Graves when, while walking along a beach north of Chicago at the end of Touhey Avenue about four months after the sinking of the *Thal*, they suddenly saw a pair of human feet protruding from the sand! They ran to the nearest police station and breathlessly informed a desk sergeant that they had just found a human body half-buried on the beach. Detectives quickly exhumed the unidentified body, which was described as being that "of a gray-haired man,...about 35 years old," about five feet six inches tall, of stocky build, and smooth shaven. The head and face had been crushed, probably by winter ice, obscuring facial details. Although missing two upper teeth, four others contained gold fillings, indicating that "the man had been well-to-do." No papers or valuables were found in the pockets, and no distinguishing marks, such as tattoos, were found. The body appeared to have been in the water about three months. Shoes were on the feet. The police had two theories: this man had committed suicide by drowning, or he was one of the *Thal* sailors. The shoes detracted from the *Thal* theory, "as a sailor on the *Thal* would have been dressed in rubber boots and oilskin clothing unless prepared for a swim for his life, when he by all means would have taken off his shoes." The body remained unidentified.

This 1898 storm that sank the *S. Thal* inflicted various degrees of damage and destruction to several other ships. The one that received most of the media atten-

 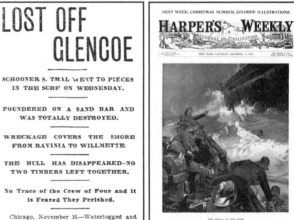

Above, left: *This 1898 court document libeling the* S. Thal *led to August Schuenemann's purchase of the vessel.* (NATIONAL ARCHIVES, CHICAGO). **Middle:** *Headlines screamed the* Thal's *loss, this one from the* **Detroit Free Press,** *Nov. 11, 1898.* (KOHL-FORSBERG COLLECTION). **Right:** *The daring rescue of the* Iron Cliff's *crew at Chicago attracted most of that storm's media attention;* **Harper's Weekly,** *Dec. 10, 1898.* (KOHL-FORSBERG COLLECTION)

tion was the stranding of the huge schooner-barge named the *Iron Cliff* at Chicago, and the dramatic rescue of the ship's crew by the local Life Saving team. The 212-foot-long ship was, much to everyone's surprise, later recovered and returned to service, lasting until 1934 when it was abandoned at Sandusky, Ohio.

Herman Schuenemann was hard hit by the death of his beloved older brother. He had planned to join him on this final run, but had fortunately remained at home to help out there just after the birth of his twin daughters, Hazel Marion and Pearlie "Pearl" Clara, on October 6, 1898. With mixed emotions that Christmas of 1898, Herman counted his blessings. In later years, just before their father's final voyage of the season, the twins would extract a promise from him that he would call them on their birthday to let them know he was safe.

Aware that this personal tragedy also placed him in a financial predicament, Herman Schuenemann made the difficult decision to leave his new, twin babies temporarily alone with their mother and older sister, while he attempted to salvage their Christmas earnings. He owned the 130-foot-long *Mary L. Collins*, but unlike the previous year, he had no extra money to pay for a captain; he instead sailed the ship himself with as large a crew as he could afford, not returning to Chicago with his time-sensitive cargo until Dec. 5th (1898), later in the year than he would have liked.

Herman carried on the shipping business after his brother's untimely death. At the end of each year, he brought his tree-laden ship to the same southwest corner of the Clark Street bridge in Chicago, tied up at the dock and sold his goods directly to the public. The jovial Herman, his blue eyes twinkling, would string festive lights from mast to mast and proclaim on his large sign, "Christmas Tree Ship. My prices are the lowest." His wife and daughters, and some friends worked in the below-deck area

Chicago Inter-Ocean, Dec. 7, 1909.
(KOHL-FORSBERG COLLECTION)

Bankruptcy documents signed by Herman Schuenemann in 1907 show that he owed a lot and owned very little. The double "nn" in Hermann is German, and likely appeared on his birth or baptismal document, making it the legal spelling.

(NATIONAL ARCHIVES, CHICAGO)

Captain Schœnemann

The original surname spelling was probably "Schonemann" with an umlaut (two dots) over the "o." German type fonts often used the joined "oe" in its place. The family had anglicized their name to "Schuenemann." With so many Nordic immigrants living in the area, the Door County Advocate *understandably invested in European type fonts.*

(KOHL-FORSBERG COLLECTION)

heated by a wood-burning stove, bending and tying wreaths out of cut greens. Before long, "Christmas Tree Schuenemann's" arrival in Chicago with a boatload of pines and boughs became a tradition marking the commencement of the holiday season.

The annual Christmas tree run was a gamble, but, fortunately, it paid well. Despite already being owner of his ship, hiring men to cut and load 5,000 to 8,000 trees and make the final run of the season could cost him $3,000 in wages and tug towing fees (for entering and departing a harbor). But the trees usually sold for 75 cents or one dollar each, with the largest pines going for ten dollars or more, so Herman could theoretically earn nearly double his expenses in sales. Despite his own financial situation being tight, he generously gave away many trees every year to churches, orphanages and poor families.

He continued to dabble in various business enterprises. A failed beerhall-like tavern project forced Herman to declare bankruptcy in a formal "Debtor's Petition" filed on January 4, 1907, showing that he owed $1,344.70 to 15 Chicago companies, nearly half of it to the Val Blatz Brewing Company. His listed assets were "one set of clothes" ($5), "one overcoat" ($5), and "one watch and chain" ($10). This commercial failure appeared to have no effect upon his maritime business ventures.

Herman Schuenemann might spend the year transporting lumber and barely making any money from his work, but that final Christmas tree run would put him safely into the profit zone. For that reason, "Captain Santa," as he became known, would cram his vessel's holds with trees and greens, then raise the ship's booms, pile more trees eight feet high covering the entire deck and lash them down. The crew would have to clamber over trees to sail the ship. Despite weather conditions on the Great Lakes being at their worst in November, that dangerous final run simply had to be made to maintain financial solvency.

When Herman Schuenemann arranged in 1910 to use the schooner *Rouse Simmons* for its first time as a Christmas Tree Ship, he was already set up in a position destined to establish "Captain Santa's" fame and legend.

FIVE

The *Rouse Simmons*

❄   ❄   ❄   ❄   ❄   ❄

The three-masted schooner, *Rouse Simmons,* slid down her launch ramp at Milwaukee and into the waters of Lake Michigan during the lazy days of late summer in 1868. Built by the shipyard of Allan, McClelland & Company and designed by the firm's mastermind, Louis Palo, for R. B. Towsley and Captain Alfred E. Ackerman of Kenosha, Wisconsin, the ship was named after a prominent industrialist (Rouse Simmons, 1832-1897) from Kenosha, a lumber businessman who had helped finance the boat -- and who, later, in 1870, became involved in the family establishment of the famous Simmons Bed Company which became noted for its Simmons Beauty Rest mattress.

The *Milwaukee Sentinel* reported on Saturday, August 15, 1868:

New Vessels -- Launches. -- The *Rouse Simmons,* one of two new vessels recently contracted for by Kenosha parties, will be launched this afternoon from the shipyard of Messrs. Allan, McClelland & Co. Her dimensions are as follows: Length overall, 127 feet; breadth of beam, 27 feet 6 inches; depth of hold, 8 feet 1 inch; measurement about 220 tons. The model of the *Simmons* combines speed with large carrying capacity, and in this respect must be considered faultless. Her entrance, though seemingly full, is nevertheless quite sharp, and her run is really beautiful. The timber used in her construction is the finest we have ever seen put into a vessel, and the manner in which it has been put together reflects the highest credit upon the builders. The cost of the new vessel, when fully completed and ready for sea, will be in the neighborhood

The first enrollment of the new schooner **Rouse Simmons** *was issued at Milwaukee on August 27, 1868.*

(NATIONAL ARCHIVES, CHICAGO)

of $17,000. She will carry three masts, fore-and-aft rigged, with square sail on foremast. Her owners are Royal B. Tousley and Capt. Akerman [sic], of Kenosha, the latter of whom will have command. The *Simmons* is designed for the lumber trade, and will ply between Manistee and Chicago.

Not noted by the press was an unusual fact about the new ship: the *Rouse Simmons* was built with TWO centerboards, unlike most ships of her type and size that carried only one. A double centerboard was built into the largest sailing vessel ever constructed on the Great Lakes, the five-masted *David Dows*, in 1881 at Toledo, Ohio, but its length of 265 feet -- double that of the *Rouse Simmons* -- warranted such a radical design addition. It is not known why the *Simmons* was built with this unusual feature. On Friday, September 4, 1868, after the interior work had been completed, the *Milwaukee Sentinel* gave a brief account of the ship's first voyage: "First Trip. -- The new schooner *Rouse Simmons* sailed from this port at a late hour Wednesday evening on her maiden trip. She has gone to Manistee for lumber."

The *Rouse Simmons*, constructed for the lumber trade on Lake Michigan, made one experimental trip carrying a load of grain to Lake Erie in October, 1868, but it was clear that the ship's cargo area was too small for it to be financially competitive in this area. She carried only 14,000 bushels of grain, while vessels built specifically for the grain trade could haul twice as much.

Working hard as one of the many Lake Michigan "lumber hookers," in her first full navigational season afloat, the *Rouse Simmons* had two accidents, both

The earliest known photograph of the schooner **Rouse Simmons** *was taken in 1884.*
(KOHL-FORSBERG COLLECTION)

in September, 1869. The vessel was driven ashore near Manistee, Michigan, but was quickly pulled off with no damage, and later that month, the ship lost its sails and gear in a storm on Lake Michigan. These represented common experiences for sailing ships at that time.

Several huge lumber companies in Wisconsin, Michigan, and Illinois operated their own fleet of ships that carried their products to various markets. One of the largest, which became Hackley & Hume of Muskegon, Michigan, acquired the *Rouse Simmons* in 1873, utilizing the vessel extensively over the next 25 years.

Chicago worked hard to rebuild its city after the Great Fire of October, 1871, and in 1872, 12,000 ship arrivals were recorded at its port, of which 75% were vessels carrying lumber. Schooners like the *Rouse Simmons* helped make Chicago not only the world's greatest lumber market, but also the world's busiest harbor.

For example, of the 143 ships listed under "Port Arrivals" in the *Chicago Inter Ocean* for May 31, 1874, 108 carried lumber, wood, or bark, and, interestingly, the list included the schooners *Rouse Simmons, Bertha Barnes, Kate Hinchman, Truman Moss, J. V. Taylor, A. J. Mowery*, and the scow *Coaster*, all destined to become Christmas Tree Ships. It was a busy time for the Lake Michigan lumber trade.

From the *Chicago Inter Ocean* on November 21, 1876, we can glean an idea of how often in a season a "lumber hooker" would have carried a short-haul cargo:

> The schooner *J. [John] V. Jones,* owned by Bigelow Brothers, lumber merchants, of this city [Chicago],...the past season, has unloaded in Chicago one cargo of ice...and *fifty-two* [italics original] cargoes of lumber, from Muskegon, Mich., making fifty-three cargoes. These cargoes have averaged 220,000 [board] feet each, and aggregate 11,660,000 feet. We venture the assertion that no other vessel has ever made as many trips in any one season from this port, or that any one *sail vessel* [italics original] has ever brought that amount of lumber into this port in one season before...through our narrow river, often so filled with vessels that a passage was scarcely possible....

The schooner, *John V. Jones,* built in 1875 at Manitowoc, measured 201 gross tons and 130 feet in length, being, in fact, very similar to the *Rouse Simmons*. But, as indicated in the newspaper article, the *Jones'* numbers were exceptional that year. The typical lumber hooker made between 30 and 40 runs annually.

The lumber trade on the Great Lakes employed thousands of men cutting and hauling trees (left) *and loading ships with sawn lumber* (right). (Kohl-Forsberg Collection)

Like the majority of Great Lakes sailing vessels in the late 1800's, the *Rouse Simmons* experienced some harsh conditions and minor mishaps, including:

> **The schooners *Rouse Simmons, Starlight, H. C. Albright, Robert Howlet,* and the *Levi Grant* arrived yesterday looking like moving icebergs.**
>
> *-- Chicago Inter Ocean,* November 25, 1881

> **The schooner *Rouse Simmons* lost its jibboom and foremast yesterday by crashing into Adams street bridge. The bridgetender had started to swing the bridge, and the power gave out when the bridge was half open. The schooner could not be stopped in time. The damage was confined to the schooner.**
>
> *-- Chicago Daily Tribune,* November 20, 1899

The crew of the *Rouse Simmons* sometimes experienced similar difficulties. Sailor John Filan fell from the masthead at 10 AM on April 29, 1872, and was severely injured. Capt. W. C. Rothwell, despondent over damage done to the *Rouse Simmons,* his first command, in November, 1875, committed suicide at Chicago's Sherman House. It had taken him a week to sail the *Simmons* from Muskegon to Chicago because, when a storm blew out his mainsail, the ship was first towed to Manitowoc, only to lose an anchor there. When found, the dead but formerly determined captain had a revolver and a new razor with him, but he had opted for death by morphine. On Friday night, June 27, 1879, Capt. Miller of the *Rouse Simmons,* while crossing the railroad track at Michigan City, Indiana, was struck by an engine, and died the next day. His body was later taken to Pentwater by train.

On May 21, 1891, the *Rouse Simmons* departed Chicago for Muskegon in the

The **Rouse Simmons** *at anchor in 1890, as close to shore as possible, taking on a load of bark transported in multiple trips on a small raft.*   (KOHL-FORSBERG COLLECTION)

company of the equal-sized schooner, the *Thomas Hume,* also owned by the Hackley & Hume Lumber Company, to pick up lumber cargoes. Both ships were empty. The seas on Lake Michigan worsened, so the *Simmons* turned around, returning to Chicago. The *Hume* pressed on and disappeared with all hands. The *Thomas Hume* was located, sitting upright in 150 feet of water, by A & T Recovery in 2003.

With the area's lumber boom declining, Hackley & Hume sold the aging *Rouse Simmons* to a man named John Leonard in 1898, and the ship joined the many "tramp schooners" drifting from port to port in search of any kind of cargo, made increasingly difficult by the new, steel steamers that were getting the jobs.

In 1903, the *Rouse Simmons,* badly broken up in a stranding at Torch Lake, was towed to Charlevoix, Michigan, and repaired over the winter. In the October, 1905, storm that sank several ships across the Great Lakes, the *Simmons,* 15 miles off Two Rivers, Wisconsin, lost her deck cargo of lumber and all of her sails and spars, with only a stub of the foremast remaining. The helpless vessel was blown across the lake, the crew fearing they were doomed, but at 2 AM, using torches, they attracted the railroad car ferry, *Grand Haven,* which took them in tow.

In 1910, the schooner *Rouse Simmons* and Captain Herman Schuenemann found each other, and that became the very first year that the *Rouse Simmons* worked as a Christmas Tree Ship. The *Door County Advocate,* in its "Items from Chicago" column, noted on December 1, 1910:

> **The schooner *Rouse Simmons*, Capt. H. Schuenemann, has arrived in port from the foot of the lake with a full load of Christmas trees, and all his friends trust that good results may be realized from the venture, as nearly two months have been consumed in the work, having left port along about October 1st. The *Simmons* is lying at Clark street bridge.**

The Rouse Simmons *at Sheboygan in an undated photo.* (KOHL-FORSBERG COLLECTION)

Concern over the use of old sailing ships posing potential dangers to the lives of their sailors was expressed on June 29, 1896, in the *Chicago Daily Tribune*:

> ...No one ever looks after a sail vessel. Not one in ten has any life-saving appliances worth the name. In one week last fall the crew came into port with the oilcoth which had covered the kitchen table nailed over the bottom of the lifeboat to keep the water out. When the South Chicago life-saving crew went to the wreck of the schooner *John Raber,* off the Indiana shore, their pikes went so far into the rotten sides they could not be released without bringing a part of the boat with them.
>
> Two old, abandoned tubs, which had lain in the river a couple of years, started out to bring in Christmas trees. The foot of a sailor went through the deck of one, and the rigging of the other was carried away a few miles from port.... "They were literally floating coffins, but the government inspectors could do nothing [since these ships were not steam vessels]....
>
> "I have been surprised at the lack of life-saving appliances on board most of these craft. Sailors apparently don't care whether there is a life-preserver around. They would never leave a boat for such a trifling thing as life-saving apparatus. Nor do they care much about the rottenness of the vessel, so long as they do not get into trouble...."

But for years, the warnings went unheeded, and no inspection of aging schooners was mandated. The *Rouse Simmons,* calculated to have brought over 200 million board feet of lumber to Chicago during her long career, left Chicago on October 3rd, 1912, to pick up her final shipment, a cargo that was destined to establish the ship's fame and legend.

This photo of the **Rouse Simmons,** *taken in the autumn of 1912 by William P. Larson, the Waukegan, Illinois, lightkeeper as the lumber-laden ship entered that harbor, was made into a postcard and sold by Larson to the public.* (KOHL-FORSBERG COLLECTION)

SIX

The Final Voyage

WOODEN HULLS WILL DISAPPEAR

Many Losses Among Resuscitated Craft Expected This Season.

...It is generally expected that many wooden hulls will disappear this season, because of the excessive rush of trade on the lakes many of those that have been out of commission for several years, were put in again and have earned their owners some money. The underwriters point out that in most cases where one of these goes down, the actual damage in money is not much worse than when a steel freighter goes on the rocks and twenty plates have to be removed.

-- *Duluth* (Minnesota) *Herald,* November 5, 1912, nearly three weeks before the *Rouse Simmons* sank in Lake Michigan.

Herman Schuenemann and his crew, busy cutting evergreen trees at the northern end of Lake Michigan for the lucrative Christmas market in Chicago, undoubtedly missed reading the above warning about aging, wooden ships when it appeared in a newspaper at the western end of Lake Superior. It is unlikely that Herman's crew of tree harvesters near Manistique, Michigan, had a chance to read <u>any</u> newspapers at all while they toiled in the remote north woods for several weeks.

The old schooner, *Rouse Simmons,* working as steadily as she could find work in the lumber trade, had ended the 1910 and 1911 seasons with successful, final runs to northern Michigan, returning to Chicago with full cargoes of Christmas trees which sold for a considerable profit. Herman Schuenemann hoped to repeat the success of the previous two years, and he planned, once again, to make his trees available at dockside on the Chicago River by Thanksgiving Day at the end of November.

Captain Schuenemann neither outrightly owned, nor completely leased, the schooner *Rouse Simmons*. In 1912, he held a one-eighth ownership interest in the vessel, as did his partner, Captain Charles C. Nelson. However, the dominant three-quarters owner was a man named Mannes J. Bonner who lived at St. James on Beaver Island in northern Lake Michigan.

Schuenemann was also, technically, not the captain of the vessel during that tragic year's-end run with Christmas trees; the 68-year-old widower and part-owner, Captain Nelson, had been coerced out of retirement by Herman Schuenemann to master the ship in late 1912. Nelson had to promise his daughter that this would be his last voyage before re-entering retirement for good.

A year earlier, in early October, 1911, while heading up to Manistique for Christmas trees, Herman Schuenemann and Charles Nelson had stopped at Sturgeon Bay, Wisconsin, to have the *Rouse Simmons* recaulked, as she had begun leaking badly while in a gale off Two Rivers on their way north. The following year, they did not have any maintenance work done on the ship prior to reaching Thompson's Pier, southwest of Manistique, Michigan, in October, 1912.

Thompson, Michigan, had its start when the Delta Lumber Company in 1888 named its newly-platted lumber and harbor community after its owner and president, E. L. Thompson. At its peak in 1907, this community, with a population of 900, featured three churches (Catholic, Methodist, and Swedish Lutheran), four saloons, six schools, a hotel, a boarding house, a general store, a barber shop, and a hospital with three doctors and a midwife, as well as a lumber dock reaching far out into Lake Michigan servicing the many ships that loaded and transported a for-

The **Rouse Simmons** *was allegedly photographed on its way north to gather Christmas trees in Oct., 1912. This photo appeared in the* **Manitowoc Daily Herald** *on December 14, 1912 -- but where is Schuenemann's large deck cabin?* (KOHL-FORSBERG COLLECTION)

tune in lumber. Unfortunately, when the area's timber lands became increasingly depleted, the town followed suit. By 1919, only 150 residents remained.

In 1912, when the *Rouse Simmons* and its crew reached Thompson, they could see that it was a community in decline. But they themselves had arrived there on a style of ship that was in even greater decline. They worked on board a wooden schooner which was clearly obsolete, a vessel that had, decades ago already, been left in the dust on the freshwater seas by larger, stronger and faster ships made of steel and powered by steam. It felt as if life had suddenly become much faster, fueled by imaginative creations that appeared to leap from pages of science fiction books, inventions like automobiles, aeroplanes, and wireless. Old-time sailors could see, with their own eyes, that by 1912, commercial sailing ships on the Great Lakes were already rare. Schooners had become nostalgic sights that turned heads wherever they passed. For the most part, the sailors on the *Rouse Simmons* had lived and worked through an era that was nearly gone, and they tried hard to hold on to their fading lifestyle, annually hoping that it would last just another year.

So the men, their ship, and their acquaintances in Thompson had much in common as they worked together to supply Chicago with Christmas trees. Herman Schuenemann, grateful for the assistance the people of Thompson gave him and his crew towards accomplishing their goal, always gave the children treats before his ship set sail.

Friday, November 22, 1912

After cutting and loading trees for several weeks, Capt. Schuenemann and his crew departed Thompson's dock on Friday, November 22, 1912, heading south

*The lumber community of Thompson, Michigan, reached its peak in the very early 1900's, but was already in its decline due to receding timber stands when the **Rouse Simmons'** crew cut Christmas trees here in 1912.* (KOHL-FORSBERG COLLECTION)

towards Chicago with the *Rouse Simmons* seriously loaded, if not overloaded, with Christmas trees and boughs. Sharing crowded space with these yuletide symbols of joy and happiness were Capt. Herman Schuenemann, Capt. Charles Nelson, and somewhere between eight and fifteen sailors and hired tree cutters. The vagaries of the *Simmons'* final crew list, with several unemployed sailors having been picked up in impromptu fashion along the Chicago waterfront by Capt. Schuenemann for the trip north, was compounded by the last-minute addition at Thompson of several lumberjacks seeking to hitch a ride on the schooner to Chicago.

How many evergreen trees were packed on board the *Rouse Simmons* for her final voyage? The reported numbers vary considerably.

Surely, by 1912, Herman Schuenemann had a very good idea of how many trees he could logically sell from his boat in the short time slot of only a few weeks before Christmas. We have no record of precisely how many sales people, family members included, Herman employed, or could employ, on the limited deck space of his schooner -- although it would appear evident from the many personal remembrances that everyone who went there to buy a Christmas tree also wanted to purchase it directly from "Captain Santa" himself. Hypothetically, if a Christmas tree were sold from the deck of the *Rouse Simmons* at a steady rate of one tree every three minutes for 12 hours a day -- a very optimistic rate of sales -- it would take 20.8 days to sell 5,000 trees. That would rule out considerably larger cargoes

An additional wooden structure to warehouse more Christmas trees was built by Herman Schuenemann on the deck of the **Rouse Simmons**, *taking up all the space between the masts at each end of the ship.* (KOHL-FORSBERG COLLECTION)

of 10,000 trees, or, heaven forbid, 27,000, as reported by some newspapers. Considering the length of time it took to select, cut, and load trees onto the ship, in addition to the labor costs, plus the growing conservational concern over receding forests in the northern Great Lakes, Herman Schuenemann would not have had his workers cut more trees than he felt he could realistically sell.

Yet Schuenemann's addition of a large, tall, specially-constructed cabin between the foremast and the mizzenmast (the first and third masts), to house extra Christmas trees, shows his optimism about the Chicago market. The *Chicago Inter Ocean*, on December 5, 1912, stated, "Captain Schuenemann constructed a deck-house running from the foremast to the cabin, using between 15,000 and 20,000 feet of green lumber. It was eleven feet high and would offer great resistance in a gale." This deckhouse was not new or experimental; he had built similar structures on previous Christmas tree ships he sailed. But it made operating the ship difficult. Strong winds could easily catch this increased freeboard, making it difficult to keep the ship on course. And with this cabin built from rail to rail, the only way a sailor could move along the length of the ship was to clamber over the top of the cabin and hope that the sail and boom would not unexpectedly swing and knock him overboard. But once the ship reached safe harbor, the Schuenemanns and other workers would clear out some trees, position tables and chairs and a wood-burning stove inside, and have a comfortable place where they could make wreaths and other Christmas decorations.

Not all of Schuenemann's original crew returned to Chicago with him. Just before the ship sailed out of Chicago in early October, rats had left the ship. Only one crewmember named Hogan Hoganson took serious note and acted on this su-

Left: *Sailor Hogan Hoganson had seen rats leave the* **Rouse Simmons** *just before the ship departed Chicago harbor. When he saw the overloaded schooner at Thompson, he remembered the rats -- and, forsaking his pay, took a train back to Chicago.*

Right: *Several newspapers, including the* **Chicago Record-Herald** *on December 5, 1912, printed the "rats" story.* (KOHL-FORSBERG COLLECTION)

SHIP LEFT BY RATS LOST IN LAKE WITH ALL HANDS ABOARD

Schooner Rouse Simmons, With Christmas Trees, Believed Wrecked

MAN WHO QUIT BOAT TALKS

Seaman Says Superstition and Heavy Cargo Drove Him From His Berth.

perstition. In his own published words:

> **It was the rats that gave me my first 'hunch' that trouble was ahead for the *Rouse Simmons*. The rats had deserted the ship while it lay in the Chicago harbor. And all the way across the lake, as we sailed for our cargo, the old saying had been ringing in my head - - 'The rats always desert a sinking ship.'...Well, when we had filled the hold with Christmas trees at Manistique, we were ordered to pile up a deck load of the saplings. The load grew and grew, and still they had us piling more and more trees on top. Finally I protested to Captain Nelson, telling him that if we struck heavy weather, the boat would be too topheavy to weather it. But the captain seemed to think he knew more about it than a seaman, and ordered us to pile more trees on deck. Then I quit. Captain Schuenemann, the owner of the cargo, told me I would get no money unless I stuck for the cruise, but I had some money and so I took a train for Chicago. Here I am -- and the others?**

Capt. Nelson had also observed the departing rats at Chicago, and told Capt. George DeMar of the Chicago Harbor Police that he feared this was a bad omen. At least one eyewitness claimed to have seen rats leaving the *Rouse Simmons* just prior to the ship's departure from Thompson on her final voyage.

Capt. Schuenemann knew a storm was approaching. He also felt the onset of cold weather, and he did not want to be trapped and frozen in at Thompson over the winter. More than anything, many Chicago families were counting on him to bring them Christmas trees! Despite the superstitious belief that it is bad luck to sail out of a port on a Friday, and with sailors on shore shaking their heads in disbelief, the overloaded *Rouse Simmons* left Thompson, Michigan, on Friday, November 22nd, 1912, in an attempt to outrun the descending storm and the upcoming winter, and

to reach Chicago by Thanksgiving Day, Thursday, November 28th.

Saturday, November 23, 1912

The newspaper in Sturgeon Bay reported on November 28th, 1912, that

> **A storm of unusual violence swept over this region on Saturday, accompanied by rain and snow. It continued thru out the night and the following day with unabated fury. Vessels were driven to shelter in friendly harbors....**

But the *Rouse Simmons* had reached no friendly harbor. The dark, menacing skies had quickly broken into a violent storm. With temperatures dropping, choppy seas rising, and increasing winds howling, the trees in the *Rouse Simmons'* leaky holds became wet and heavy, while those in the cabin and on the deck bore the increasing weight of frozen spray.

When last seen afloat by other human beings on Saturday, November 23, 1912, the *Rouse Simmons* was flying a distress flag and seemingly careening out of control, even under partial sail, quickly down the lake off Kewaunee, Wisconsin.

The Life Saving Station at Kewaunee sighted the struggling ship, but the crew had only rowboats on hand, and knew they could never catch up with the schooner. Aware that the Two Rivers Life Saving Station farther south had a gasoline-engine-powered life saving boat, they telephoned Two Rivers.

The "General Remarks" in the daily Life Saving Report at Kewaunee on November 23, 1912, show the concern expressed over the offshore schooner (the original spelling, punctuation and grammar remain intact in these reports):

> **Telephone OK. Mustered Crew for fire Drill only, raining. Crew were cleaning House. About 2:50 P.M. Lookout reported a sch. flying a Flag at half Mast. Immediately took the Glasses, and made out that there was a distress signal. The schooner was between 5 and 6 miles E. S. E. and blowing a Gale from the N. W. Thinking that she was in need of a Tug as much as the Life-Savers, I went to order the Gov. [U.S. Army] Tug *Industry* but she had left in the fore-noon for Sturgeon Bay. By that time snow set in and we lost sight of her.**
>
>

Nelson Craite
>
> [Added on a separate sheet]: **Knowing that the Two Rivers station was equipped with a Power Life-Boat, where they would be in a better**

Watchers at the Kewaunee (Wisconsin) Life Saving Station saw the schooner in distress several miles off shore, but, because they had only rowboats at their disposal, they contacted the nearby Two Rivers Life Saving station. (KOHL-FORSBERG COLLECTION)

position to get along side and board her, I telephoned to Capt. Sogge telling him to get out and meet her, but they failed to locate the schooner, either by not coming north far enough, or not standing Out in the Lake far enough, as it was snowing.

Capt. Sogge at the Two Rivers Life Saving Station wrote the details of his actions in response to the telephone call he received about the distressed schooner:

At 3:10 P.M. The Capt. of the Kiwaunee Life Saving Station called me by Telephone, stating a Schooner under short sails headding South and under good heaway and about 5 miles out from his Station was displaying a flag halfmast.

The wind was blowing strong W.N.W. and fair weather for the Schooner to make good allong this Shore and I expected the shooner would be near Two Rivers Point about 5 P.M. At 3:20 P.M. I launched the power lifeboat and at 6:20 I was about 13 miles north of this Station, but nothing to be seen of the Schooner. At this time weather got very misty and started snowing heavy.

I considered the schoner had change her course and steered E. out into the Lake. I turned about and came home, arrived at the Station 8 P.M. I called up the Capt. of Kiwaunee Station and informed him our results.

What happened on the murky lake that blustery afternoon was clear: As the

Members of the Two Rivers (Wisconsin) Life Saving crew headed out into the unfriendly waters of stormy Lake Michigan in their gasoline-engine-powered lifeboat, which was similar in size to the Two Rivers rowboat pictured above. (KOHL-FORSBERG COLLECTION)

Two Rivers Life Saving crew raced to assist the *Rouse Simmons* in worsening weather, the schooner disappeared. Then a blinding snowstorm shrouded the lake, leaving the would-be rescuers struggling to return to their port. But for the crew of the *Rouse Simmons*, the struggles were over.

Sunday, November 24 to Thursday, November 28, 1912

Under smooth sailing conditions, it was normally a three-day run from Manistique or Thompson at the north end of Lake Michigan to Chicago at the southern end. But in November's bad weather, it could easily take twice as long. Barbara Schuenemann and her three daughters awaited the arrival of the *Rouse Simmons*, becoming increasingly concerned as the week progressed. Finally, on Thanksgiving Day, the 28th, they announced that the ship was overdue, and they asked the public for any information about possible sightings of the vessel.

The weekly newspaper at Sturgeon Bay jumped the gun, incorrectly reporting

> **The schooner *Rouse Simmons*, Capt. Schueneman [sic], recently arrived at Chicago with a cargo of Christmas trees, there being about eight carloads in the lot, all of which he expects to dispose of before the holidays. It was a difficult thing to get the trees this season owing to the swamps and thickets in the northern part of Michigan being flooded with water. The trees are gathered in the vicinity of Manistique.**

Unfortunately, the same severe storm in which the *Rouse Simmons* found itself had proved fatal for two other vessels and their entire crews on Lake Michigan. The 69-foot-long motor schooner, *Three Sisters*, built at Fish Creek, Wisconsin, in 1901, tried to ride out the storm while at anchor in Green Bay off Red River on Saturday. On Sunday morning, efforts to rescue the three men proved futile, and all succumbed to the bitter cold. Meanwhile, on the other side of Lake Michigan, the 35-foot-long, 38-ton fish tug, *Two Brothers*, built in 1891 at Sheboygan, went out on Sunday in severe weather conditions off Pentwater, Michigan, to lift nets. The three crew members quickly saw the folly of their action. Upon returning to Pentwater, their boat was suddenly cast upon the pier by an unexpected, huge wave, slid back into the water, and all the men were drowned in front of shocked witnesses watching helplessly from shore.

Captain Sogge of the Two Rivers Life Saving station wrote a detailed report of his crew's efforts to assist the distressed schooner off their shores.

(NATIONAL ARCHIVES, CHICAGO)

Friday, November 29, 1912

Newspapers in Chicago, Milwaukee, and Detroit printed short articles stating simply that the schooner, *Rouse Simmons,* was overdue on Lake Michigan. But the crew of the schooner, *Resumption,* reported seeing an overturned yawl boat floating in the lake off Kewaunee on this date. The hope was that the yawl had been torn from the ship by the storm, and that the ship itself had found safety in a secluded cove or bay. Regardless of the number of people on the missing ship, whether 10 or 18, the single lifeboat that the *Simmons* carried could not have held everyone who was on board, even if it were the lower number. Hogan Hoganson had stated that

> "The old schooner never carried such a thing as a lifeboat. There was one boat on board which was 'sculled' back and forth to land the crew, but so far as any real lifeboats were concerned, they never had any on board. That one boat would hold fifteen men in the Chicago River, but it wouldn't have held one if we had ever launched it in rough weather."

Saturday, November 30, 1912

One of the six daily newspapers in Chicago reported that the *Rouse Simmons* had been sighted off Baileys Harbor in Wisconsin's Door County peninsula, temporarily quieting fears over the crew's safety. "The ship is five days overdue, but is expected to arrive in Chicago some time today."

Sunday, December 1, 1912

The ship did not arrive, and no word about the location of the *Rouse Simmons* reached Chicago.

Monday, December 2, 1912

Another day passed in which neither the *Rouse Simmons* nor any information about its location arrived, causing increased concerns among the members of Herman Schuenemann's family, but the four women stayed strong and hopeful.

WATCH FOR LOST SCHOONER.

Life Savers Look Out for Lumber Boat and Crew Which Were Due Here Yesterday.

The life saving crew was asked last evening to keep watch for the lumber schooner Evelyn Simons, supposed to have arrived here yesterday morning. No word has been received from the schooner since it left northern Michigan with a cargo. The boat is commanded by Capt. H. Nelson, and has a crew of six. Mrs. Nelson, wife of the captain, accompanied him on the trip.

SCHOONER OVER DUE

Fear Felt for Safety of Rose Simmons and Crew.

CHICAGO, Ill. Nov. 28.—The schooner Rose Simmons, Capt. Scheuneman, with Christmas trees, is reported here as three days overdue. The schooner carries fourteen hands and sailed from Thompson, Mich., on Nov. 21.

Very short newspaper announcements, such as these two in the **Chicago Daily Tribune** *and the* **Milwaukee Sentinel** *on November 29th, quickly snowballed into longer, detailed articles as the* **Rouse Simmons** *remained lost.* (KOHL-FORSBERG COLLECTION)

Tuesday, December 3, 1912

Bad news about the "Christmas Tree Schooner," now many days overdue, reached the public in numerous newspapers. Reports indicated that a quantity of Christmas trees had washed ashore at Pentwater, Michigan, on the eastern side of Lake Michigan, having been blown across the lake by strong northwest winds.

Wednesday, December 4, 1912

Headlines today included "No Hope for Boat and Her Crew of 16" (*Detroit*

Chicago Inter Ocean	*Chicago American*	*Manitowoc Daily Herald*
Capt. H. Schuenemann	Capt. H. Schuenemann	Capt. H. Schuenemann
Capt. Charles Nelson	Capt. Charles Nelson	Capt. Charles Nelson
Steve E. Nelson, mate	Philip Bauswein	Alex. Johnson, First Mate
Frank Carlson, sailor	Frank Carlson	Philip Bauswein, sailor
Sven Inglehart, lumberer	Andrew Danielson	Ray Davis, sailor
Albert Lykstad, cook	Jack Johnson	Frank Faul. sailor
Charles Nelton, sailor	Philip Larson	Conrad Griffin, sailor
Ingvald Nyhous, sailor	Albert Lykstad	Edward Hogan, sailor
William Oberg, lumberer	Stephen Nelson	Edward Minogue, sailor
Gilbert Svenson, sailor	Engwald Newhouse	"Stump" Morris, sailor
	John Pitt	John Morwuski, sailor
	Gilbert Svenson	Edward Murphy, sailor
		Greely Peterson, sailor
		George Quinn, sailor
		Frank Sobata, Sailor
		George Watson, sailor

Numerous newspapers printed **Rouse Simmons** *crewmember lists, sometimes with names differing considerably, as these three samples indicate.*

Left: Simmons *sailor Philip Bausewein was scheduled to be married upon his return from this trip, but when he failed to come home by Thanksgiving Day, both his fiancée and his mother visited waterfront towns north of Chicago to try to find word about the* **Rouse Simmons.**

Right: *When Albert Luxtad (pictured) signed on as the* **Rouse Simmons'** *cook, his lifelong friend and shipping 'mate,' Engwald Newhouse, also joined the crew.* (KOHL-FORSBERG COLLECTION)

Phillip Bausewein.

News), "Find Wreckage from Schooner" (*Duluth Herald*), "Ship Carrying Christmas Trees Goes Down in Lake" (*Toledo Blade*) and "Christmas Ship Goes to Bottom" (*Milwaukee Journal*). Inquiries made at numerous coastal towns in Wisconsin yielded no news of the missing ship. The *Chicago Record-Herald* reported that the family was not giving up hope, and that Mrs. Schuenemann "maintains that there is no cause for alarm...and [she] added that the newspapers were showing the greatest worry." One newspaper gave one of the earliest published bits of misinformation about the *Rouse Simmons*, namely that its Christmas trees "have constituted an annual cargo [for the *Simmons*] for 30 years." In reality, it was only the *Simmons'* third year as a Christmas tree ship. The Lake Seamen's Union reported that the government revenue cutter, *Tuscarora*, had left Milwaukee that morning "in search of the missing craft."

Thursday, December 5, 1912

One newspaper reported that "the hatches of a ship" (probably meaning hatch covers) and a large number of Christmas trees had washed ashore near Two Rivers. Others offered "mute evidence" that the ship "lies at the bottom of Lake Michigan off Two Rivers point, twelve miles north of [Manitowoc]," this evidence being the fact that fishermen pulled up pieces of evergreen trees in their nets some five miles north of Two Rivers. The wife of Captain Nelson was still reported as being

The 178-foot-long U. S. revenue cutter, Tuscarora, *built in 1902 at Richmond, Virginia, searched for the* Rouse Simmons *from Dec, 4-10, 1912.*   (KOHL-FORSBERG COLLECTION)

part of the crew, although she had died a few years earlier. Several other newspapers carried interviews with the critical Hogan Hoganson, who had left the vessel before the *Simmons* departed Thompson. One of the Milwaukee papers compared the *Simmons'* loss to those of the schooner *Thomas Hume* in 1891 and the steamer *Chicora* in 1895, both disappearing in storms with all hands and no trace of the ships or bodies ever being found. But the revenue cutter, *Tuscarora*, received a communication from the steamer *George W. Orr*, stating that they had sighted the missing schooner at 7 A.M. Wednesday about three miles off shore, heading for Racine. In addition, one newspaper printed one subheading with one word that offered a spark of optimism: "Hope <u>Nearly</u> Abandoned."

Friday, December 6, 1912

A letter written by Capt. Schuenemann and mailed prior to his departure from Thompson, and revealed by the office of a teaming contractor in Chicago, stated that part of the evergreens and Christmas trees was being shipped by rail because Schuenemann "could not get them all on the boat," proof that the *Rouse Simmons* was very likely overloaded when she left the dock at Thompson. An investigation into the *George W. Orr's* claim of having seen the *Rouse Simmons* "heading for Racine" proved it to be groundless. The revenue cutter, *Tuscarora*, continued to

THE "ROCKS"

On December 9th, 1912, this hardhitting cartoon was printed in the **Detroit Times.** *Normally, such cartoon commentaries were drawn in response to a late-season, loss-of-life shipwreck, with the wealthy steamship owner caring only for his profit and nothing for his crew. While no steamer sank under such conditions in late 1912, this image could, generically, be applied to the loss of the schooner,* **Rouse Simmons,** *showing the severe price sometimes paid for fast profits at year's end.* (KOHL-FORSBERG COLLECTION)

search the lake without results. In Chicago, at the Lake Seamen's union headquarters at 574 West Lake Street, more than 30 sailors gathered, talked of their missing comrades, and generally abandoned hope for the *Rouse Simmons* and its crew. Finally, the *Detroit News* reported that 700 Christmas trees, "doubtless from the wreck of the *Rouse Simmons*," had floated ashore at Kewaunee, Two Rivers, and Sturgeon Bay (even though Sturgeon Bay is on the inside of Green Bay and not on the Lake Michigan side; they likely meant the entrance to the Sturgeon Bay Canal), and that the trees were being offered for sale by whoever found them. The same article, as well as one published in the *Milwaukee Daily News,* noted that the body of a sailor, about 50 years old and believed to be from the *Rouse Simmons*, had washed ashore near Pentwater, Michigan.

Saturday, December 7, 1912

While at least two Lake Michigan newspapers identified the body found at Pentwater as probably being that of Steve Nelson, the mate on the *Rouse Simmons*, several others, including the *Detroit News*, were already one step ahead: the body had been positively identified as that of Tony Johnson, a crew member of the fish tug, *Two Brothers*, that sank the same weekend as the *Rouse Simmons*. Meanwhile, the *Tuscarora*, having swept the lake between Waukegan and the Sturgeon Bay Canal for any sign of the *Rouse Simmons*, reported finding "no wreckage anywhere." Fears were expressed that two other schooners, the *Minerva* and the *George A. Marsh*, were lost with all hands in the recent severe gale on Lake Michigan.

Sunday, December 8, 1912

The lumber schooner, *Minerva*, covered with ice, her canvas frozen, and with several of her booms broken, finally reached Chicago, ten days overdue. Word was received that the missing schooner, *George A. Marsh,* was also safe in a port of refuge. The Schuenemann family members hoped for news that the *Rouse Simmons* had limped into a port -- any port. Their hopes were again raised when two men who had been making lake observations on November 24th from atop a huge lumber pile at Port Washington, Wisconsin, claimed to have seen the *Rouse Simmons* battling its way through the waves, heading south. But this was soon disproven.

The shipping season drew to a cold close. On December 10th, the ice-encrusted lumber schooner, *J. V. Taylor,* finally reached Chicago after a nine-day struggle from Alpena, Michigan, on Lake Huron. The *Taylor* had ducked into seven different harbors whenever the biting cold hurricane blew its worst. The schooner, *Butcher Boy,* floated into Milwaukee days overdue, looking like an iceberg.

But no word arrived of the *Rouse Simmons* being safe in a remote anchorage.

The revenue cutter, *Tuscarora*, went out of commision for the winter on December 10th, when 30 of the crew were discharged. The 110-foot-long revenue cutter, *Mackinaw*, then searched for the *Simmons*, but, under orders from the treasury department, abandoned the search on December 17, 1912.

Even before that date, the Schuenemann women knew what had to be done.

Although Milwaukee scuba diver Kent Bellrichard was alone when he found an unidentified shipwreck in Lake Michigan in late 1971, he did a dive on it after securely lodging the small boat's anchor into the wreck. Conditions at depth were very dark, and his underwater light failed, so he had to feel his way around the shipwreck. He managed to tie a long line with a floating marker buoy to the wreck, and returned a week later with John Steele, at which time they were able to identify the shipwreck as being the tragic **Rouse Simmons.** (PHOTO BY CRIS KOHL)

Kent Bellrichard located the wreck of the schooner **Rouse Simmons** *on Saturday, October 30, 1971, in 165 feet of water off Two Rivers, Wisconsin. He had borrowed fellow shipwreck hunter John Steele's boat and electronic equipment and gone out on the lake on an overcast, foggy day. Above, John Steele and Kent Bellrichard closely watch the electronic printout of a more modern vintage sidescan sonar while searching for a shipwreck in Lake Superior in July, 1997.* (PHOTO BY CRIS KOHL)

John Steele organized a search for a Lake Superior shipwreck in July, 1997, with long-time wreck hunting friends Kent Bellrichard (seated), George West (in red), Steve Radovan, and Jim Brotz (far right). Unknown to everyone, this was John's farewell hunt before selling his boat and equipment, and retiring from the lakes. (PHOTO BY CRIS KOHL)

A shipwreck show at the Milwaukee Public Library auditorium in November, 1996, featured presentations by (left to right) *Cris Kohl, John Steele, and Kent Bellrichard.*
(PHOTO BY JOAN FORSBERG)

In 2002, Kent Bellrichard appreciated receiving a photograph of the unique alligator figurehead located on another one of his 1970's shipwreck discoveries which, like the Rouse Simmons, *was also a three-masted schooner, namely the* Dunderberg, *lying in 155 feet of Lake Huron water. The underwater photo of this 1868 shipwreck was taken by Cris Kohl.* (PHOTO BY JOAN FORSBERG)

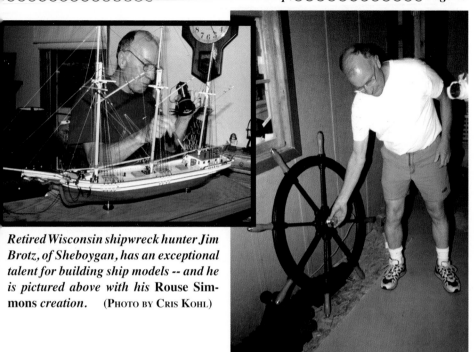

Retired Wisconsin shipwreck hunter Jim Brotz, of Sheboygan, has an exceptional talent for building ship models -- and he is pictured above with his **Rouse Simmons** *creation.* (Photo by Cris Kohl)

Above, right: *When the ship's wheel, and its attached steering rod and frame (weighing over 400 pounds total) from an old schooner was brought up in a commercial fishing net in 1999 one-and-a-half miles away from the wreck of the* **Rouse Simmons,** *it was taken to Wisconsin State authorities. They made a careful selection in choosing Jim Brotz to work on the wheel's restoration. This photo of Jim and the wheel, nearing completion in 2002, was taken in his basement workshop.* (Photo by Cris Kohl)

Below: *Inside the wheel's brass sleeve in the hub was stamped the date of manufacture: 1868, the year the* **Rouse Simmons** *was built. Scuba divers in 1971 wondered what had happened to the* **Simmons'** *wheel, since it was not on the wreck or close by it. Apparently a falling boom sent the wheel and its heavy components to the lake bottom, and for 1.5 miles, the unsteerable ship and its terrified crew were taken on a wild Great Lakes version of a "Nantucket sleighride" before tragically sinking. Today this wheel is on display at the Rogers Street Fishing Village Museum at Two Rivers, Wisconsin, along with other* **Rouse Simmons** *artifacts.* (Photos by Cris Kohl)

Divers Tom Pakenas and Steve Radovan prepare to dive to the deep wreck of the Rouse Simmons, *the Christmas Tree Ship.*

Steve Radovan descends.

Tom Pakenas shines his light on the Rouse Simmons *as he nears the stern deck on his first dive here.* (Photos by Cris Kohl)

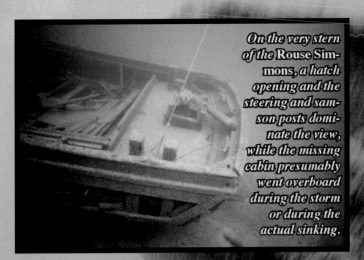

On the very stern of the Rouse Simmons, a hatch opening and the steering and samson posts dominate the view, while the missing cabin presumably went overboard during the storm or during the actual sinking.

Dropping under the Simmons' transom reveals the mostly-embedded rudder and various shipwreck debris.

(PHOTOS BY CRIS KOHL)

The largely intact hull of the **Rouse Simmons** *displays the strength with which it was constructed in 1868. The decking, however, all the way from the missing stern cabin* (the area seen at right) *to the windlass at the bow, is badly fragmented.* (PHOTO BY CRIS KOHL)

Sheboygan diver Steve Radovan follows the **Rouse Simmons'** *starboard rail towards the bow, carefully examining the incredibly broken-up decking of this 44-year-old ship, and savoring the many unobstructed views of the cargo below deck.* (PHOTO BY CRIS KOHL)

It has been suggested that perhaps Capt. Hermann Schuenemann removed many of the deck planks and used them in the construction of the special midship housing he built to compress and protect the extra trees the vessel carried in 1912. (PHOTO BY CRIS KOHL)

Visiting divers who peer past the decking debris can see many examples of the **Rouse Simmon's** *final cargo of evergreen trees -- mostly without the "green" parts, except for the deeply buried ones -- still stowed below.* (PHOTO BY CRIS KOHL)

Above: *Aquatic visitors to the wreck of the* **Rouse Simmons** *marvel at how full the cargo area remains; more trees were on the deck.*
Left: *Another view of the badly broken deck.*
Below: *Thousands of silt- and mussel-covered skeletal Christmas tree trunks and branches remain in the hold.*   (PHOTOS BY CRIS KOHL)

Above: *The bow decking, supporting a windlass with heavy chain, appears to be little damaged compared to the rest of the deck.*
Right: *Lighting up the windlass and its chains.*
Below: *Parts of masts, booms, and bowsprit lie forward, a hint that the ship's bow came into hard contact with the bottom.* (PHOTOS BY CRIS KOHL)

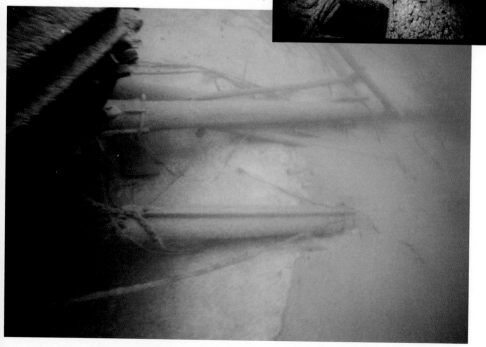

The impressive view of the wreck from forward of the Rouse Simmons' bow shows balanced catheads on port and starboard sides, and draped chains descending to the lake bottom. The port bow anchor and its long chain were dropped to try to anchor and save the ship. Anchor and chain lie mostly embedded in the soft lake bottom, running about 160 feet out from the hull. (PHOTO BY CRIS KOHL)

Above: *In late 2000, the US Coast Guard cutter* Mackinaw *helped revive the annual appearance at Chicago of a ship carrying Christmas trees.*
Right: *A tradition upheld: the* Mackinaw *brought free trees for needy families in Chicago, thanks to Chicago's Christmas Ship committee.*
Below: *The stern deck served as the transportation platform for the 1,000 trees.* (PHOTOS BY CRIS KOHL)

A Christmas Tree Ship memorial service, an annual event in early December at Navy Pier's "Captain at the Helm" statue, is held prior to the unloading of the trees, usually done by youth group volunteers. Dave Truit (3rd from left above) co-authored the first Christmas Tree Ship play with other members of the Underwater Archaeological Society of Chicago. (Photos by Cris Kohl)

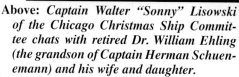

Above: *Captain Walter "Sonny" Lisowski of the Chicago Christmas Ship Committee chats with retired Dr. William Ehling (the grandson of Captain Herman Schuenemann) and his wife and daughter.*
Right: *Socializing after the ceremonies.*
Below: *In the first* Mackinaw's *pilot house, Ohio diver/historian Joyce Hayward interviews Capt. Joseph McGuiness, while Canadian diver Dave Mekker shoots video for a documentary.* (PHOTOS BY CRIS KOHL)

Left: *The long-established von Stiehl Winery of Algoma, Wisconsin, produced special Christmas Tree Ship commemorative wines, starting in the mid-1990's, honoring the town's native son, Captain Herman Schuenemann, who was born in Algoma in 1865 and sailed his first ships out of that harbor.* (COURTESY OF THE VON STIEHL WINERY)

Right: *The von Stiehl Winery also produced a special "Cherry Blossom Blush" wine commemorating the Christmas Tree Ship. The winery generously donated a portion of the proceeds to Chicago's Christmas Tree Ship Fund.* (COURTESY OF THE VON STIEHL WINERY)

Many people have done significant work to help keep the Christmas Tree Ship story -- and spirit -- alive in modern times: 1. Author Rochelle Pennington wrote two books about the Christmas Tree Ship, one for children and one for adults. 2. Ruth Gibson Fleswig wrote her children's book based upon the story of her mother's disappointment in 1912 when the **Rouse Simmons** *failed to bring the customary cargo of Christmas trees to Chicago. 3. Fred Neuschel wrote two history books about the Christmas Tree Ships. 4. Folksinger/Songwriter Lee Murdock wrote songs about the* **Rouse Simmons** *as well as the Coast Guard Cutter* **Mackinaw** *and its role in reviving the Christmas Tree Ship tradition, often performing those songs at the Navy Pier ceremonies.* (PHOTOS BY CRIS KOHL)

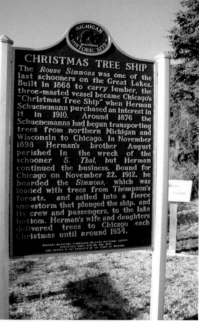

CHRISTMAS TREE SHIP

The *Rouse Simmons* was one of the last schooners on the Great Lakes. Built in 1868 to carry lumber, the three-masted vessel became Chicago's "Christmas Tree Ship" when Herman Schuenemann purchased an interest in it in 1910. Around 1876 the Schuenemanns had begun transporting trees from northern Michigan and Wisconsin to Chicago. In November 1898 Herman's brother August perished in the wreck of the schooner *S. Thal*, but Herman continued the business. Bound for Chicago on November 22, 1912, he boarded the *Simmons*, which was loaded with trees from Thompson's forests, and sailed into a fierce snowstorm that plunged the ship, and its crew and passengers, to the lake bottom. Herman's wife and daughters delivered trees to Chicago each Christmas until around 1934.

Above: *A historic marker and an interesting circle of historic plaques were set up by the state of Michigan in 2006 at Thompson, Michigan, the* **Rouse Simmons'** *last port of call where the ship loaded its heavy cargo of Christmas trees at the extreme northern end of Lake Michigan.* (PHOTO BY CRIS KOHL)

Above right: *The tragic story of the Christmas Tree Ship has become an important part of Michigan's history, as well as that of Wisconsin and Illinois.*

Below: *The several informative plaques at Michigan's "Christmas Tree Ship" marker relate the story of the* **Rouse Simmons,** *plus this region's lumber history and the story of the short-lived community of Thompson, Michigan, which started in 1888 as a lumber town, reached a peak of 900 people in 1907, but was reduced to only 150 by 1919. Today a dozen buildings remain at this former busy harbor.* (PHOTOS BY CRIS KOHL)

Captain Herman Schuenemann
1865 - 1912

"The story of the Rouse Simmons...is the Great Lakes' unique entry in the catalogue of all things Christmas." -- Cris Kohl, Wreck Diving Magazine, *Issue 4 (2004).* (PHOTO BY CRIS KOHL; INSET IMAGE FROM THE CHRISTMAS TREE SHIP MEMORIAL AT THOMPSON, MICHIGAN.)

SEVEN

Aftermaths -- Carrying On

❄ ❄ ❄ ❄ ❄ ❄

Barbara Schuenemann had lost her husband, Herman, to Lake Michigan, and 20-year-old Elsie and her younger sisters, the twins, Hazel and Pearl, recently turned 14, had lost their father. In addition, all of the family's money had been invested in the cargo of the *Rouse Simmons,* and the lake took the cargo, as well as the ship, from them. They knew they had to act quickly to try to recoup their financial losses.

Initially, as reported by one newspaper on December 9, 1912, Elsie spoke about her plans "to get another boat" and then go "back to Michigan and get an

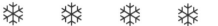

Christmas Tree Captain's Daughter Sells Greens From Spot Where Father Reaped Harvest in Former Years

THE SUBSTITUTE CHRISTMAS SHIP ONEDA.

MISS ELSIE SCHUENEMANN DAUGHTER OF THE CAPTAIN OF THE ROUSE SIMMONS.

The Schuenemanns stayed in the Christmas Tree Ship business, with oldest daughter Elsie usually being the public representative. These photos appeared in the **Chicago Record-Herald** *on December 12, 1912.* (KOHL-FORSBERG COLLECTION)

even bigger cargo of spruce and balsam saplings than my father loaded onto the *Rouse Simmons*." Realistically, it was impossible to load up another ship full of Christmas trees from the north woods, sail back to Chicago, and sell them in time for Christmas. But Elsie's optimism and determination made her the local media darling, while her strong statements probably masked her real pain of loss and desperation about the future. Occasionally she even drifted into disbelief that her father was dead, and that he, the crew, and the *Rouse Simmons* must be on one of the "islands in Lake Michigan; desolate tracts of land [as] they are...."

The *Chicago Inter Ocean* described Elsie's situation most sympathetically:

> **In a dingy little room at South Water and Clark streets, a lone window overlooks Chicago river. Yesterday there sat a beautiful, golden haired, sad eyed girl. She was weaving Christmas garlands.**
> **Now and then her fingers would halt their work and the glance of her sad, blue eyes would look toward Lake Michigan, where her father perished, and tears would fall upon the garland in her lap....**

The press gave conflicting reports about the family's plans, perhaps indicative of the Schuenemanns' own chaotic state initially. On December 10th, one Chicago newspaper reported that Mrs. Barbara Schuenemann was so "stricken with grief at the first news that her husband probably was lost, she became ill. Grief made her hysterical...." On that same day, another Chicago newspaper described her as planning to "charter the steamer *Relief* and sell Christmas trees from the boat at the *Rouse Simmons'* old dock, foot of Clarke street."

What happened was that the W. C. Holmes Shipping Company, for which Herman Schuenemann had reportedly once worked, put one of their ships, the old schooner *Oneida*, "a schooner similar in appearance to the *Rouse Simmons*, except for the Christmas tree cabin which Capt. Schuenemann had built," at Elsie Schuenemann's disposal. Staying in Chicago, it would be docked at the usual Clark Street location, reportedly selling the Christmas trees "picked up from the *Rouse Simmons* wreckage," plus a carload of trees and greens that Captain Schuenemann had shipped by rail to Chicago from the Michigan woods because there had not been enough room for them on board the *Simmons*.

With the loss of the *Rouse Simmons* and its cargo, plus the money owed to the crew and the wood-cutters, the Schuenemanns reportedly had debts of more than $5,000, every penny of which Elsie promised to repay. People flocked from all parts of the city to the *Oneida* to buy trees and wreaths, so many, in fact, that Elsie "advertised for additional help to make wreathing and prepare trees for market." However, on the day after Christmas, the *Chicago Record-Herald* reported that, despite many of the trees going unsold, the plucky Barbara Schuenemann strongly stated, "We will continue next year, for our fight is to save our home."

As a "Finis to Capt. Schuenemann's Twenty Year Epic," on Christmas Day, 1912, the *Chicago Daily Tribune* wrote:

A little woman in black and a talkative small boy in a blue suit were among the passengers yesterday on a Clark street car. As the car approached the south end of Clark street bridge, the boy exclaimed:

"Mamma, mamma, the Christmas ship is in."

"Be quiet, child," the woman enjoined.

"See, there's a Christmas tree," the boy continued, pointing to a large, storm torn spruce lashed to the bridge railing, where for many years it had been customary to display in late November and early December the Christmas trees and greens brought in annually by water from northern Michigan.

"Hush, child," the parent insisted. "There's crepe on the Christmas tree, and the brave sailors are drowned in Lake Michigan, lost in the storm."

The mourning for the missing sailors lost in the storm had already begun when, even before Christmas, words were received that allegedly had been written by one of them. On December 13th, 1912, newspapers reported the finding of a message, written on a leaf torn from a ship's log book, in a bottle near Sheboygan:

Friday. Everybody good-bye. I guess we are all through. Seas washed over our deck load Thursday. During the night the small boat was washed over. Ingvald and Steve fell overboard Thursday. God help us. Herman Schuenemann.

The 138-foot-long, 55-year-old **Oneida** *took the place of the missing* **Rouse Simmons** *in 1912, with trees sold from her decks in the Chicago River.* (KOHL-FORSBERG COLLECTION)

Since the actual message never materialized to be shown to Mrs. Schuenemann, for handwriting verification, historians are divided regarding its authenticity. It was common practice among pranksters in that era, even in tragic cases involving loss of life, to send out phony messages supposedly written in the final moments of a doomed ship's life. Based upon their content, some notes were easily labeled fake, while others, such as this one, became more speculative. The people named in the message were certainly on board the *Rouse Simmons* -- "Ingvald" being Ingvald Nyhous (or Engwald Newhouse on some lists), while "Steve" was probably Steve Nelson, the ship's mate. However, the reference to "Thursday" makes no chronological sense, since the ship had left port on a Friday and sank the very next day. In a desperate state of mind on board a sinking ship, the author of the note, already calendar-confused by having worked in the wilderness for seven weeks, where the daily calendar didn't matter, as each day's work was exactly the same, could understandably have written the wrong day of the week. However, Capt. Schuenemann was focused on reaching Chicago by Thanksgiving Day, Thursday, November 28, 1912, so he knew exactly what day it was. Also, knowing his personality, he would have included a personal message to his family in such a note.

More cynical observers deemed the note to be a hoax, either a cruel attempt by someone to extort money from the widow in return for that "authentic" note, or a sensational attempt to sell more newspapers. In fact, at least one Wisconsin newspaper deemed the emotional farewell note to be a hoax -- a message "which originated in the fertile imagination of the Chicago papers. Captain Dionne of the

FIND MESSAGE FROM DEAD CAPTAIN OF THE SCH. SIMMONS

CHRISTMAS SHIP LOST TWO OF CREW OVERBOARD BEFORE IT FOUNDERED ON LAKE NEAR THIS PORT SAYS MESSAGE

(By Associated Press)
SHEBOYGAN, Wis., Dec. 13.—Writ-

schooner in distress was sighted–off Kewaunee and for which the Two Riv-

In mid-December, a message allegedly written by Herman Schuenemann on the doomed **Rouse Simmons** *was found in a bottle near Sheboygan.* (KOHL-FORSBERG COLLECTION)

life-saving station at that point [Sheboygan] says there is no truth in the report [of a message in a bottle having been found] whatever." (*Sturgeon Bay Advocate*, December 19, 1912). The *Chicago Record-Herald* was another newspaper that, on December 14, 1912, denied the existence of such a message. If it really was a journalist's hoax, then writing down correctly two names of people who actually were on board the *Rouse Simmons* would have been a simple matter of referring to one or two of the published lists of the names of the missing. Even someone who was not a journalist could have done that.

As was their tradition at the end of the calendar year, various Great Lakes newspapers that carried marine columns, published statistics, and sometimes even detailed lists, of the maritime accidents and losses for that year just passed. The *Detroit Times*, for example, on December 14th, wrote "Thirty-five lives were lost in navigation on the Great Lakes during the season now closing....The *Rouse Simmons*...carried down with her 16 men, else the list of fatalities for the season would have been comparatively small...."

The last boat of the season to enter Chicago harbor before ice locked it up for the winter was the schooner *Butcher Boy*, on December 18, 1912. Coincidentally, the captain of that vessel had been at South Manistique, Michigan, when the *Rouse Simmons* departed from nearby Thompson nearly a month earlier. The *Chicago Record-Herald* reported these recollections on December 19, 1912:

> **"When we saw the *Simmons* beating out," said Captain August Hansen of the *Butcher Boy* last night, "I said to the others: 'Captain Schuenemann must be in a terrible hurry to get those Christmas trees to market. I wouldn't go out into this storm for all the trees the *Mauretania* [a huge trans-Atlantic ocean liner] could carry. Those boys will be lucky if they don't go to the bottom.'**
>
> **"The *Rouse Simmons* beat out on Friday. There was a heavy head sea running in. There was sudden, nasty weather, about the most sudden I remember. We lay to through Saturday and part of Sunday, and when we did clear we had to run under double reefs and then lay to three days in the lea [sic] of Plum Island** [at the tip of Wisconsin's Door County peninsula].
>
> **"We didn't see anything of the *Rouse Simmons*, but if the *Butcher Boy* couldn't stand up against the weather I know the *Simmons* couldn't, for it was an older schooner and the deckhouse full of Christmas trees fore and aft made it unseaworthy.**
>
> **"When we made Milwaukee last Thursday the schooner was covered with ice and was down by the head badly. I couldn't remember when I've seen the lake ice up more quickly."**
>
> [Authors' note: The three-masted, 155-foot-long schooner, *Butcher Boy,* was the exact same age as the *Rouse Simmons*, having been built in 1868 at Depere, Wisconsin, and the ship was reportedly scrapped in 1917.]

In early January, 1913, an empty trunk with the names "*Rouse Simmons* -- J. E. Lathrop" washed ashore on the beach near Kewaunee. The three boys who found it

-- Gordon and Dewey Dishmaker and Art Fiala, discovered that, despite its being empty, its weight made it too heavy to carry, so they broke off the part bearing the names and took it into Kewaunee.

Also in January, 1913, Captain T. Bernsten of the railroad carferry *Ann Arbor No. 5* told his tale of seeing the *Rouse Simmons* about five miles off Kewaunee at about 2 P. M. on that fateful Saturday, November 23, 1912:

> **She was flying no signals of distress as far as they could see, although she was about half a mile from them at the time. The vessel appeared to be listed badly and they thought something was wrong but as there were no signals visible they did not deem it necessary to go to her, never thinking but what she would make harbor in safety. She was carrying reefed foresail, staysail and standing jib, and was heading up for the shore. They wondered at the time why she wasn't heading for Chicago, as she had fair wind....**

In mid-May, 1913, a second message in a bottle from the doomed *Rouse Simmons* was reported found:

> **R. Simmons went to bottom with cargo and crew after jamming sunken ice, crushing front of boat.**
> **Michael Rattary, night watchman**

This message was clearly fraudulent; there was no evidence that any person by that name was on board the ship, or that any such position as "night watchman" was a job title used on the schooner. No reports of floating ice in the lake existed for November 23, 1912, and, years later, after the wreck of the *Rouse Simmons* was found, the "front of the boat" showed no "ice" damage whatsoever.

In July, 1913, eight months after the ship's loss, a third message in a bottle, purportedly from someone on the *Rouse Simmons*, was found by a boy named Frank Lauscher, the son of a fisherman, just north of the mouth of the Sturgeon Bay Canal. Written roughly in pencil, it read:

> **Nov. 23, 1912. These lines were written at 10:30 p.m. Schooner *Rouse Simmons* ready to go down about 20 miles southeast of Two River [sic] Point between 15 and 20 miles offshore. All hands lashed to one line. Good-bye. Capt. Charles Nelson.**

Local marine men at the time considered the note to be the true "last word" from the *Simmons*. Today, it is not known what ultimately became of this note.

The stalwart Schuenemann women, after waiting and hoping that Herman, the crew and the ship would be found safe in some hidden anchorage, gradually accepted the reality of their loss and determined to proceed with their lives. A tough breed sprung from hardworking immigrant stock, the Schuenemanns stoically carried on the tradition of selling Christmas trees from an old ship at Chicago's Clark

Street bridge, just as they knew Herman would have wanted them to do.

A year after her tragic loss, Barbara Schuenemann spent eight weeks in northern Michigan supervising the cutting of Christmas trees. She loved the smell of pines, the clear, starry nights, the sound of axes chopping -- in fact, she described it as one long holiday for her. The main reason, however, that she loved this work was for the comfort it provided -- she felt that her late husband, Herman, was with her. This is what he would have been doing at that time of year had he remained alive. In an emotional article in the *Chicago Record-Herald* in late 1913, Barbara revealed that her husband had told her three years earlier, "If anything should happen to me, Barbara, I want you to keep on bringing Christmas trees to the kids of Chicago." She felt happy in honoring her late husband's request.

A year after the *Rouse Simmons* disappeared, Elsie Schuenemann appeared at a newspaper office with a tribute she had written:

SCHUENEMANN -- CAPT. HERMANN [sic].

Uncertain is the life of those who go down to the sea in ships. Of the many brave men who spend their lives on the sea, there are some who sail away from port, never again to be heard from by their dear ones. Such an [sic] one was our beloved husband and father, who, together with the fourteen men under his command, lost his life a year ago today, when his ship, the *Rouse Simmons*, foundered in Lake Michigan. At the time the cargo of the *Rouse Simmons* consisted of Christmas trees, being brought to Chicago to bring Yuletide cheer to thousands of children. In a similar way our husband and father spent his life -- in doing what he could to further the happiness of others. In reverence, honor, and love do we today pay tribute to his memory, and to that of the brave men who met death with him.

His Wife and Children.

In late 1913, Elsie and Barbara Schuenemann posed with Christmas trees on the deck of the J. V. Taylor. *The 46-year-old, 125-foot schooner, despite lasting for another 15 years before being abandoned at Racine, Wisconsin, in 1928, was apparently used as a Christmas Tree Ship only this one year.* (KOHL-FORSBERG COLLECTION)

At the same time, Elsie proudly announced that "There will be another Christmas ship in Chicago this year. Mother is now up in northern Michigan superintending the cutting of the Christmas trees."

The *Sturgeon Bay Advocate*, in its "In and Around Chicago" column, on December 11, 1913, reported that

> **The schooner *J. V. Taylor* will spend part of the winter laying at the Clark street bridge, having been loaded with Christmas trees by Mrs. Schuenemann, wife of the captain of the ill-fated Christmas tree schooner, *Rouse Simmons*. The trees were brought in from the woods of northern Michigan by rail and transferred to the *Taylor*.**

Although their Christmas trees were conveyed to Chicago from the north woods by train, the Schuenemann women managed to find an available schooner to use on the waterfront as a traditional platform for their sales.

The *Detroit Free Press,* on December 5, 1913, under the heading "Builder of Schooner *Rouse Simmons* Dies," related the news that Capt. Alfred Ackerman, 88 years old, a good friend of prominent Chicagoans Marshall Field and Joseph Medill, died at his home at Twin Lakes, Wisconsin, and that he had been master of the schooner *Rouse Simmons*, which "was built by him."

In December, 1913, following the example of New York City, Chicago set up, in Grant Park, its first municipal Christmas Tree, 35 feet high and decorated with

The Schuenemanns used the schooner, **Arendal,** *as their Christmas Tree Ship in Chicago in 1914. For some seemingly unfair reason, this fine but old vessel, which had sailed the Great Lakes for 43 years when it was sold for use on salt water in 1916, was abandoned somewhere on the East Coast in 1918.* (KOHL-FORSBERG COLLECTION)

electric lights. At 6 P.M. on Christmas Eve, Mayor Harrison pressed the button that lit up all the lights, the Chicago Band played, grand opera stars sang, and the Paulist choir and a Swedish chorus performed. The giant evergreen was supplied by Chicago tree dealer F. J. Jordan, a "former partner of Capt. Schuenemann."

On the day after Christmas, 1913, the three Schuenemann daughters, "with a stiff wind whipping their clothing," stood at the lakefront and cast wreaths of holly and evergreen into Lake Michigan in memory of their father, then "the three knelt and offered [a] prayer for the crew, of whom no trace has ever been found."

The Schuenemanns repeated their Christmas Tree Ship tradition for many years afterwards, continuing to do a man's work at a man's job, and succeeding in a man's world where women did not yet have the right to vote. In late 1914, the Chicago press reported that Barbara Schuenemann, who had "been in the Michigan woods near Manistique since early in September,... safely piloted the boat [the schooner *Arendal*] down the treacherous lake," being met at the dock by daughter Elsie, "who has charge of the wreath making girls." (However, another report indicates that, in 1914, Barbara Schuenemann chartered the schooner *Fearless* -- a 126-foot-long, two-master that was built one year earlier than the *Rouse Simmons* and was reportedly abandoned shortly after 1914 -- as a Christmas Tree Ship, and that both she and Elsie spent weeks in the north woods supervising the work.)

In 1915, newspaper accounts declared that Elsie and her mother spent several weeks in the forests of Schoolcraft County, Michigan, arranging the cutting of the trees, which were then conveyed by sail to Chicago, arriving on December 1st on board the schooner, *C. H. Hackley,* of which Elsie was made the "honorary captain." Elsie reportedly "again has leased the big freight room controlled by the Indiana Transportation company, and into this she expects to put a big shipload of Christmas trees for sale to Chicagoans."

A November 21st, 1916, article states that Barbara Schuenemann had "loaded her schooner with Michigan pines for Chicago's Yuletide and will soon sail."

In 1917, Barbara and her daughters utilized the 50-year-old **Minnie Mueller,** *which had lain abandoned in the Chicago River since 1915.* (KOHL-FORSBERG COLLECTION)

On November 22, 1917, "with big, Christmasy snowflakes clinging to her mastheads, the Christmas ship *Minnie Mueller* came into the Clark street dock.... She brought from the Michigan woods the first cargo of Christmas evergreens."

The year 1919 saw dramatic changes, a good one for the Schuenemann family but other changes not so good for their Christmas tree sales in Chicago:

> ...persons who for years have bought their trees from the Schuenemann family's Christmas tree boat at the Clark street dock will not find them in their old familiar place.
>
> Mrs. Barbara Schuenemann...returned from the northern woods yesterday, bringing with her by freight train thousands of trees to make the hearts of Chicago children glad.
>
> For twenty-seven years Capt. Schuenemann had a boat load of trees at the Clark street dock each Christmas and since his death his widow has continued the business.
>
> Yesterday she was informed that Harbor Master James J. McComb had granted the privilege to other parties, as she had failed to apply early enough. Mrs. Schuenemann had intended to charter a boat for the trip, as she sold her boat to the government two years ago, but when docking arrangements were altered she changed her program.
>
> Mrs. Schuenemann's Christmas trees will go on sale today at 323 North Clark street, where her daughter, Elsie, now Mrs. Arthur Roberts, known as "The Christmas Tree Girl," will be in charge.
>
> Mrs. Roberts said yesterday: "Christmas trees will be much cheaper this year. Last year profiteers charged from $5 to $20 each, and many poor people had to go without them. This year trees will sell from 50 cents to $1.50 each."

Unrelated to the Schuenemanns' work that year, the ship, *Liberty*, brought 100,000 baby spruces to Chicago from Escanaba, Michigan. This may have been the "other parties" to whom the Chicago Harbor Master had granted riverfront space. At any rate, the lack of an old ship at the usual Clark Street bridge dock in 1919 marked the beginning of a brief decline in media interest in the Christmas tree work that the Schuenemanns continued to do each year.

An unusual event occurred in early April, 1924. A commercial fisherman made a startling catch in Lake Michigan off Two Rivers -- snagged in the meshes of the fishing net he pulled up was an oilskin-covered wallet. It contained personal cards of Capt. Herman Schuenemann and newspaper clippings about the Christmas trees he had brought to Chicago over the years. All of the contents were not only readable, but amazingly intact. Tellingly, the wallet contained no money.

Dr. William Ehling, grandson of Herman Schuenemann, recalls that the recovered wallet was kept by his family and that, on special occasions during his childhood, it was exhibited to family members. But the wallet has since disappeared.

The accidental discovery of Herman Schuenemann's wallet briefly brought the *Rouse Simmons* into a small spotlight in 1924, but it was clear that the story of the most tragic Christmas Tree Ship was being forgotten. The *Chicago Herald and Examiner*, in reporting the story of the recovered wallet on April 8, 1924, gave the date of the schooner's loss as "November 24, 1914" -- off by two years and a day.

By 1929, this media memory loss had grown worse. In reporting the catastrophic sinking of the steel freighter, *Andaste*, on September 14th, one newspaper commented that "Two other freighters, the *Chicora* and the *Rouse Simmons*, went down in Lake Michigan after similar experiences, each with twenty-five men aboard. The *Chicora* sank in 1895 and the *Rouse Simmons* in 1910." This date for the *Simmons'* sinking was still two years off the correct date, but now the sailing ship was called a "freighter" and the crew number had reached "twenty-five."

Later the following month, when the railroad carferry, *Milwaukee*, sank with the disastrous loss of all 52 on board, the *Rouse Simmons* was again referenced, this time sinking "in December, 1911."

Barbara Schuenemann remained faithful to the Christmas tree tradition made famous by her late husband. For the next 20 Christmases after the loss of the *Rouse Simmons* in 1912, she and her daughters, twins Pearl and Hazel, and particularly the oldest, Elsie, supervised the transport of fir trees and their sale along the Chicago River, or, when ships became scarce, from a small shop near there, until Barbara died at the age of 67 on June 15, 1933. Her obituary dubbed her "The Christmas Tree Lady" and "Woman Skipper of Christmas Tree Boats." Her headstone in Chicago's Acacia Cemetery bears both her name

THE CURSE OF THE WRONG YEAR

The well-known story of the *Rouse Simmons* and its tragic loss on November 23, 1912, has appeared in books, magazines and newspapers in varying lengths and degrees of detail. This tale, however, appears to be cursed by a wicked Time Hex, as many versions of the story, even some written by popular authors and printed by respected publishing giants, gave the wrong year of the vessel's loss.

For example:

"...the *Simmons*...sailed...on November 25, 1913...." -- *Lore of the Lakes* by Dana Thomas Bowen (1940), p. 170.

"...On November 25, 1913, the vessel set sail from Thompson harbor" -- *Lake Michigan* by Milo Quaife (1944), p. 253.

"...That was on November 25, 1913. The next day,...the *Simmons* was sighted off Sturgeon Bay...." -- *Great Lakes Shipwrecks and Survivals* by William Ratigan (1960), p. 38.

"*Rouse Simmons* -- Freighter, November 26, 1913...." -- *Directory of Shipwrecks of the Great Lakes* by Karl E. Heden (1966), p. 23.

"...on the morning of November 27, 1913,...." -- *Great Stories of the Great Lakes* by Dwight Boyer (1966), p. 100.

"..sank...on November 25, 1913...." -- *Namesakes 1910-1919* by John Greenwood (1986), p. 28.

"...Two weeks after the 'big blow' [of November 8-9, 1913],...the schooner *Rouse Simmons*...sailed from Thompson...on November 25...." -- *White Hurricane* by David G. Brown (2002), p. 201.

Various newspapers, ranging from those in big cities along Lake Michigan to some in small harbor towns of Ontario, since the 1970's, and even into the new millenium, printed "1913" instead of "1912" in their *Simmons* articles. It might just be true that "History repeats itself, and historians repeat one another."

Since the end of World War Two, hundreds of newspaper and magazine articles have raised public awareness of the **Rouse Simmons** *story.* (KOHL-FORSBERG COLLECTION)

and that of her husband Herman (although no body from the *Rouse Simmons,* including his, was ever recovered). An image of a fir tree, symbol of their common goal, stands in the headstone's center with the two names (see photo on page 48).

In 1933 and 1934, the Schuenemann daughters continued the family work of selling Christmas trees, now from a Chicago lot as had become their custom. But their marriages and their children were good reasons for focusing attention to their homes; they were also deep into the Great Depression -- so the tradition ended.

The *Rouse Simmons* story went dormant until Christmas of 1944, at which time, with the end of the Second World War in sight, the *Chicago Tribune* printed a story about the 1912 Christmas Tree Ship. By the early 1950's, several newspapers each year reminded people of the Christmas Tree Ship tradition with an article, often interviewing people who had known the ship and the Schuenemanns.

During this time in mid-century, Chicagoan Theodore S. Charrney (May 29, 1909 - February 13, 2007) became wholly fascinated by the story of the *Rouse Simmons*, and spent many years researching that one ship, on occasion writing articles about it. Always hoping to publish a book about the Christmas Tree Ship, but unable to find a publisher, he typed a massive, two-volume history of the vessel comprising hundreds of pages -- the most complete research done on the *Rouse Simmons* -- and placed copies with various Chicago institutions.

Artist Charles Vickery (July 16, 1913 - September 22, 1998), with four popular paintings, did much to raise public awareness of the *Rouse Simmons* story -- although he did not live to see the largest rise in popularity of this story and his art.

Researchers, writers, musicians and artists have added to the public's awareness of the Christmas Tree Ship -- but from different perspectives than when a Milwaukee scuba diver actually found the wreck of the *Rouse Simmons* in 1971.

EIGHT

The Shipwreck Discovery

When we hear the words "scuba diving," we probably picture those exciting and irrepressible images of the underwater world first shown to us on television by Jacques Cousteau, the 1940's inventor of the aqualung, or "self-contained under-water breathing apparatus," s.c.u.b.a. for short. We watched his films, fascinated and mesmerized, and yearned to explore for ourselves that subaquatic world of warm, tropical saltwater, with 200 feet of underwater visibility, brightly-colored coral reefs and tens of thousands of rainbow-hued fish of endless varieties.

Shipwrecks also appeared in our collective imaginations, influenced by pi-rates-and-treasure books for children like *Peter Pan* (1911) by James Barrie, *Treasure Island* (1882) by Robert Louis Stevenson, and R. M. Ballantyne's *The Coral Island* (1858), and we likely carried those early images with us into our adult years. Except for the fact that they were underwater, shipwrecks, in our minds, still looked very much like regular ships, sitting upright and intact, perhaps on a bit of a jaunty angle, with torn sails wafting lightly in the current while suspended from the upright masts, with all of the vessel's nautical components remaining precisely in their expected positions. Of course, there was always a human skeleton draped over the ship's wheel, and bodies bobbing about below deck.

In reality, salt water organisms would completely destroy any exposed wood within a year. Intact wooden shipwrecks quickly collapse and disappear. Gone would be the wooden hulls, the masts, the ship's wheels. Human bodies would also quickly vanish, eaten by salt water marine life. Skeletons, too, would soon dissolve into nothingness due to the corrosive effects of salt water.

The Great Lakes are very different. Missing are the colorful coral reefs and rainbow-hued fish. Absent are the tropics' warm waters, where swimmers and div-ers need wear little more than a bathing suit to explore the underwater world.

The freshwater, inland seas are, for the most part, cold all year long; severe winters can cover them with ice as far as the eye can see, and during the summers, only the shallow shorelines and surface waters warm up enough for comfortable swimming wearing only swimwear. The predominant underwater colors in the wa-ters of the Great Lakes are hazy shades of green. Comparatively little aquatic life is normally seen by subaquatic explorers in the inland seas.

But the Great Lakes have one very unique advantage: they contain the best-preserved shipwrecks in the world!

These very cold, fresh waters have helped conserve more than 6,000 ships that have been wrecked in the Great Lakes since the year 1679. They are so well preserved that they have been called "ice water museums," and today, the shipwrecks in the Great Lakes, seen as being truly unique on this planet, down to even the most miniscule of their components, are protected by state and provincial laws.

For a century, hardhat divers were the well-known "rock stars" of the Great Lakes. The dangerous work they did, for which they were usually paid quite handsomely, made them unique and adventurous figures in an otherwise drab world. From the 1840's until the 1940's, hardhat divers in the Great Lakes found plenty of work, mostly on shipwrecks (which occurred with alarming frequency), to make their lives comfortable and their names, such as Johnny Green, Elliot Harrington, William Baker, James Quinn, Peter Falcon, and James and Tom Reid, respected household words. But with the development of electronics like depth sounders and radar in the 1930's, shipwrecks dramatically decreased in numbers, and eventually the few commercial hardhat divers working in the Great Lakes after World War Two were employed by gas companies specializing in submerged gas wells.

But after World War Two, the new, affordable invention called "scuba" for exploring the underwater world gradually became available in the Great Lakes. Gone was the costly, heavy equipment necessary for hardhat diving. Gone were the limitations of the long hose attached to the surface-supplied air source.

Because the most exciting things at the bottom of the Great Lakes are its many shipwrecks, a special breed of scuba diver developed in that region. Unlike in the tropics, where scuba equipment was initially used to spear fish and gather shelled marine life (with ultimately devastating results to the coral reefs), Great Lakes scuba divers found and explored shipwrecks. It was very normal, in the early years of scuba, to bring up shipwreck artifacts so that non-divers could also see them, and, fortunately, many of these items ended up in museums.

But unlike their brethren in the tropics, Great Lakes scuba divers had to insulate themselves against the cold waters of the inland seas, and one-quarter-inch wetsuits -- jacket, pants, boots, hood, and gloves -- felt restrictive and confining, and were also very difficult to put on, and later, to remove. The rubberized hoods and gloves were particularly uncomfortable and awkward, but they were a vital necessity for a person wishing to explore these historic shipwrecks. The extensive, insulative suit for diving the cold Great Lakes remains a necessity today.

In scuba's early days in the Great Lakes during the 1950's, very few shipwreck locations were known. The remains of ships in shallow waters could be seen from the surface, making it easy to find, and return to, them. Shipwrecks in water deeper than 60 feet were generally in better condition than those in the shorelined shallows, which were damaged by waves and surface ice, but it took a fair amount of searching to find deeper shipwrecks. Bottom time limitations also exist, with the standard rule being that a scuba diver can stay at 60 feet for 60 minutes (presuming he didn't run out of air sooner) without risking a serious case of the dreaded "bends," or decompression sickness. As the depth increases, the amount of allowable diving, or bottom, time decreases. At a depth of 100 feet, a diver can stay only 25 minutes. Ever since formal scuba dive training agencies started in the late 1950's in the Great Lakes, the recommended maximum sport diving depth has been 130 feet. For exploring deeper than 130 feet, scuba diving gets into the realm of "technical diving" and becomes dangerous compared to sport diving.

It was into this new and exciting world of 1950's Great Lakes shipwreck diving that a teenager from Milwaukee and a 30-something banker from Waukegan enthusiastically entered. They both quickly became intensely interested in researching, finding and diving on shipwrecks. Because the early diving community on Lake Michigan was small and close-knit, the paths of these two shipwreck divers eventually crossed.

Kent Bellrichard was only 17 when he became a scuba diver in 1959, and he was hooked immediately. He then spent a few years working as a sonics technician in the Coast Guard before transferring the skills he learned there into a civilian job as a high frequency sound technician at Milwaukee's Ladish Company. He was working there when he started seriously researching and hunting for Lake Michigan shipwrecks.

Armed with information about the general location where local commercial fishermen had been snagging their nets on an underwater obstruction, Kent eventually found the wreck of the historic steamer *Vernon*, which sank in a storm on October 29, 1887, tragically with only one survivor from the 42 people on board. Kent located this deep shipwreck, sitting in 205 feet of water six miles east of Rawley Point Lighthouse, on July 12, 1969. He was now a successful wreck hunter!

July, 1969, was also the same month that a "mystery schooner" was ambiciously raised by a team of scuba divers, led by Frank Hoffman, from a depth of 105 feet in Green Bay. The ship was successfully brought up without any damage to it, and made a triumphant entry into Marinette, Wisconsin, harbor. Eventually identified as the *Alvin Clark,* which had gone down in an 1864 storm with three lives lost, this recovered ship, at the time the oldest merchant vessel afloat, raised the general public's awareness of the region's extensive maritime history.

The year 1969 proved significant for other shipwreck discoveries. On August 8th, a group of Sault Ste. Marie scuba divers found the wreck of the schooner *B.F. Bruce* in the St. Marys River. Among those divers was a young man named Tom Farnquist, who, 17 years later, became the driving force behind the establishment of the Great Lakes Shipwreck Museum at Whitefish Point, Michigan.

In the spring of 1969, two well-known shipwreck hunters working together, John Steele and Gene Turner, had located the historic 1895 wreck of the steel steamship, *Cayuga,* in 105 feet of water in northern Lake Michigan.

The golden age of Great Lakes shipwreck hunting was well underway.

However, years before these 1969 discoveries, John Steele had begun researching and locating shipwrecks all around the Great Lakes. Born in 1926 the night his parents attended an opera in Chicago, John grew up to become Board chairman of the First National Bank of Waukegan, Illinois. He took up diving in 1959 at the age of 33, and was immediately hooked on wrecks. By the 1980's, his success at finding shipwrecks earned him the title "King of the Great Lakes Wreck Hunters."

Kent Bellrichard, photographed in the parking lot of a Milwaukee yacht club in 2006 while giving an impromptu interview about his shipwreck discoveries, found the **Rouse Simmons** *wreck in 1971.*
(PHOTO BY CRIS KOHL)

It was the friendship of Kent Bellrichard and John Steele that led to the discovery of the *Rouse Simmons*.

"Back in those days," recalls longtime wreck hunter Steve Radovan of Sheboygan, "we were a carefree, close bunch. One day we'd be out with Kent in his boat, searching for or diving on shipwrecks; the next day, we would all go out with John, on his boat, doing more of the same."

In late October, 1971, Kent telephoned John and asked him if he wanted to go out on the lake to dive the *Vernon* that Saturday, the 30th. John had a prior commitment, and, regretful that he couldn't go, offered Kent the use of his boat, which, at that time, was larger and more comfortable than Kent's. Kent jumped at the offer.

But he could find no one else to join him on that late-season day, so Kent went out on the lake by himself, despite the foreboding weather.

He was unable to locate the homemade buoy that he had tied to the wreck to mark the site of the *Vernon*. Knowing that John's boat was equipped with more sophisticated sonar than that aboard his own smaller craft, Kent decided to head north and search for the so-called Christmas Tree Ship. The story of that shipwreck was well-known, although, at that time, Kent was not even certain of the ship's real name. All the stories he had ever heard about it called it simply "the Christmas Tree Ship," and commercial fishermen -- those hard workers so familiar with the lake's contents, the ones who had given him the general location of the *Vernon* -- had told him the wreck probably lay in a certain area off Two Rivers. That was another spot where they had snagged their nets on something rising off the lake bottom.

"I put the sonar transducer in the water," Kent later recalled, "and started to chug north to where I thought the *Simmons* might be. I kept searching for about an hour. No targets showed up.

"The boat turned broadside and, as I was drifting northwest, I got a signal on the sonar. It sounded like a big school of fish."

The machine Kent was using was, in fact, an audio signal fish-finder, a German-built ELAC sonar. It was the affordable machine of choice in 1971.

"I put her in gear and made one pass over the top. It had started to blow pretty fierce out of the southeast, and it took over two hours to get the grappling hooks to hold so I could go down."

The first rule that a would-be scuba diver learns when he takes the course is "Never dive alone." But early scuba divers in the Great Lakes frequently broke that dive buddy rule" when they went underwater in conditions that basically separated them, forcing them to rely upon themselves if they ran into trouble, e.g. diving in swift water, such as the St. Clair River, where divers might have a challenging time trying to stay together, or on any shipwreck where the conditions were relatively dark, making it difficult to stay within sight of your dive buddy, a situation particularly true for deep shipwrecks.

Kent Bellrichard decided to dive alone from a borrowed boat on a windy, overcast day in late October to an unidentified shipwreck he had just located in 170 feet of Lake Michigan water. He suited up.

It took a long time for him to follow the grapnel line all the way down to where it was hooked into this shipwreck. A depth of 170 feet is equivalent to the height of a 17-story building. No scuba diver wants to run into problems at 170 feet, because the surface is just too far away.

Kent turned on his underwater light, and he could tell that the shipwreck had a wooden hull rather than a steel one. Before long, he recognized that the wreck was that of a schooner rather than that of a steamboat. So far, so good. Perhaps this shipwreck <u>was</u> the long-lost Christmas Tree Ship!

The flamboyant John Steele, in this early 1970's photo, loved Great Lakes shipwreck hunting. He worked at it long and successfully from 1959 until 1997 when he retired from diving at age 71. It was his boat that was used to locate the **Rouse Simmons** *in 1971, and he was the second person to dive that wreck.* (SUBMITTED BY JOHN STEELE)

Suddenly his underwater light began to fade, losing power, growing dimmer, and within half a minute, he found himself in total darkness on a deep wreck at the bottom of Lake Michigan. He felt his way along the shipwreck, fortunately making it back to the grapnel hook and its vertical rope that served as his lifeline to the surface, and he slowly and carefully, to avoid the risk of embolizing, made his ascent along that rope to the world of light and unlimited air at the surface. With difficulty, he managed to get back into the unattended boat, now bouncing wildly in the increasing winds. Kent quickly released the grapnel anchor, hauled it up, and headed towards safe harbor, anxious to tell John Steele about his discovery.

On the following weekend, lake conditions were surprisingly acceptable for November, the worst-weather month on the Great Lakes. Kent Bellrichard returned with John Steele to the newly discovered shipwreck in deep water to see if they could identify it. This time, Kent had fresh batteries in his underwater light.

Exploring the old schooner together in the underwater darkness, they almost simultaneously shone their lights on the stern's transom, and surprisingly found the vessel's name board not only still in place, but also quite legible. This shipwreck was, indeed, the *Rouse Simmons*.

The Christmas Tree Ship had just returned from the grave to the living world.

Newspapers in Milwaukee, Two Rivers and elsewhere along the Lake Michigan shoreline printed articles about the history of the Christmas Tree Ship, concluding with details of its recent discovery. Kent Bellrichard and John Steele, along with one of the skeletal, bare-trunk-and-branches Christmas trees that they had recovered from below deck on the shipwreck, posed with banker John Geilfuss of the Marine National Exchange Bank of Milwaukee -- the bank that had long been using the *Rouse Simmons* painting by Milwaukee artist Bob Heuel on their checks and which exhibited the pitiful tree -- looking far worse than Charlie Brown's pitifully drooping Christmas tree -- in the bank's lobby, with great public interest!

Early in his diving career, already a firm believer in educating the public about maritime history, John Steele said, "If you dive with a crowbar, you dive alone, but if you dive with a camera, you can take a thousand people with you."

He and Kent both used professional 16-millimeter movie cameras -- and expensive, unforgiving movie film -- to produce a well-received documentary about the *Rouse Simmons*. John used a Kodak K100 movie camera in an aluminum housing, with four Ikelite rechargeable underwater lights, while Kent utilized a Swiss Bolex RX16 movie camera in a clear plastic Ikelite housing with Farralon lights.

A Chicago newspaper in late 1912 had described the schooner *Rouse Simmons* as being "full of soft planks and in bad condition." Examination of the actual shipwreck today supports that description.

In all likelihood, the ship's cabin at the stern could very well have been torn off the deck by the fierce storm prior to the vessel's sinking. At the very least, the volume of air from below deck, being suddenly displaced by water rapidly entering the hull, caused the housing to burst off the ship during the sinking. As with most wooden ships that sank in the Great Lakes, the housing was no longer attached to the vessel when the wreck was located.

The tall deck load of Christmas trees inside the temporary housing, in all likelihood, would also have been swept overboard while the *Simmons* still floated. One theory put forward to explain the enormous disarray on the jumbled deck of the *Rouse Simmons* shipwreck is that the temporary housing constructed by Captain Schuenemann to hold more Christmas trees had actually been built using the

The deep wreck of the schooner, **Rouse Simmons,** *the Christmas Tree Ship:* **left,** *her starboard quarter with the remains of the mizzenmast, and* **right,** *scattered decking debris, facing the bow. See color photos on pages 84-90.* (Photos by Cris Kohl)

Simmons' own decking. But one contemporary newspaper account described the temporary cabin built by Herman Schuenemann as being constructed out of *green wood*, which the *Simmons'* well-seasoned decking definitely was not.

Trying to stabilize the ship, the crew had dropped the *Simmons'* port anchor and let out much chain in hopes of giving it enough scope to allow their survival. But it failed to save the vessel. The port anchor and chain, mostly covered by sand and silt over the past 100 years, extend about 160 feet off the *Simmons'* bow.

When the schooner sank, she hit bottom bow-first very hard and, in effect, she "shivered her timbers." The masts snapped upon impact and flew forward of the bow, from which the long bowsprit also broke off, attached to the hull now by only a few hanging chains. Practically every board comprising the deck broke off upon impact, and many of these planks remain loose in jumbled disarray on the wreck.

Even massive deck beams and hanging knees (strong, L-shaped wooden braces which firmly attached the horizontal deck to the vertical hull) were violently torn out of position. Nineteenth-century schooners that were new, or nearly new, when they sank in the Great Lakes are in immaculate condition, like the *Cornelia B. Windiate*, lost in Lake Huron during her second season and resting in 185 feet of water, compared to many old, battered shipwrecks, the *Rouse Simmons* included, which had hauled heavy cargoes for decades before their ultimate demise.

Easily viewed between the pieces of torn decking and framing are thousands of Christmas trees that were packed tightly together below deck. Today the surface trees lie denuded of needles, poking their short, bony branches up towards the surface like pointing fingers, coniferous skeletal remnants of a once joyful cargo.

Many of the *Rouse Simmons* nautical components and smaller artifacts were removed during the 1970s, including the large, heavy, wooden-stock, starboard bow anchor, two wooden nameplates, and hundreds of smaller items such as a stool, a kettle, eyeglasses, a china bowl with the letters "R. S." on it, a hand-cranked foghorn, a deadeye, and an electric lightbulb that still worked! The ship was not electrified, so this lightbulb was probably used at dockside when Capt. Schuenemann sold his trees. Removed during the 1970s before state laws made such removal illegal, these items are on exhibit at yacht clubs and museums in Milwaukee and Two Rivers, Wisconsin. The museum at Two Rivers recently acquired, as a dona-

Left, *Wreck hunter/diver Steve Radovan glides over dishevelled decking, following the starboard rail towards the bow.* **Right,** *The ship's steering post at the stern remains in place and recognizable. See color photos on pages 84-90.* (Photos by Cris Kohl)

The **Rouse Simmons'** *starboard anchor, raised by Kent Bellrichard, John Steele and some of their diving colleagues in 1973 using steel drums filled with air, and John's 26-foot boat,* **Lake Diver,** *was donated to the Milwaukee Yacht Club, which has annually festooned the anchor in bright Christmas tree lights.*
(PHOTO BY CRIS KOHL)

tion, over 200 *Rouse Simmons* artifacts from the Butch Klopp collection.

The ship's wheel was missing when the *Simmons* was discovered in 1971 This mystery was cleared up when, in 1999, a commercial fisherman accidentally pulled up in his nets a 400-pound artifact -- an old ship's wheel and its steel and iron steering mechanism -- about a mile and a half north of where the *Rouse Simmons* went down. Retired police officer, scuba diver, wreck hunter and well-known ship model builder, Jim Brotz of Sheboygan, was given the job of restoring this ship's wheel. To form new, wooden handles, Jim used old wood, namely a stray plank he had been given from the 1876 schooner *Lottie Cooper* when it was raised from Sheboygan harbor in September, 1992, and put on public display there in 1993. "You just can't buy wood like that today," he said. "The tree rings are 1/32nd of an inch apart!" The *Simmons'* wheel had been cranked hard to port, and it rusted in place in that position. Three of its wooden handles had been broken off, and two of the steel handle prongs were bent, indicating that a very heavy object, in all likelihood the ship's mizzen driver boom, had collapsed onto it, dislodging the wheel from the ship with its entire steering column. The mizzen driver boom has also never been found. When Jim painstakingly removed the rust from the wheel's brass hub, he found four patent dates on it -- and the newest one was "1868," the year the *Simmons* was launched! The discovery and identification of the *Rouse Simmons'* wheel also eliminated suspicions that Kent or John had secretly removed it from the wreck. (See page 83 for color photos of the *Rouse Simmons'* wheel.)

With the advent of the zebra and quagga mussel invasion of the Great Lakes from coastal Europe beginning in the late 1980's, and due to the mussels' prolific reproduction tendencies, rapid geographical spread, and their filter-feeding nature the waters of the inland seas have experienced increased clarity -- but at enormous ecological cost. The life cycle of a mussel colony appears to be about seven years during which time the invaders filter-clean the water, thus depleting their food supplies, and they starve to death. Before long, dirty water (their "food supply" returns, and so do zebra/quagga mussel colonies. The underwater photos of the *Rouse Simmons* that appear in this book were taken by Cris Kohl in June and July of 2004 -- at a time in the mussels' cycle when water clarity was excellent and most mussels had starved to death and their shells had fallen off the shipwreck.

The state of Wisconsin spent two weeks in 2006 doing an underwater archaeological survey of the *Rouse Simmons*, and the following year, on March 21st, the ship was added to the U. S. National Register of Historic Places.

The discovery of the actual *Rouse Simmons* wreck brought the legend to life.

NINE

The New Christmas Tree Ships

With the advent of the new millenium in the year 2000, the Christmas Tree Ship legend, which had been relegated for many years, at least in the eyes of the general public, simply to an annual newspaper article that served as a reminder that an old ship carrying Christmas trees sank with the loss of all hands in 1912 while on its way to Chicago, experienced a very visible reawakening that attracted hundreds of people to Chicago's Navy Pier.

The annual tradition of the Christmas Tree Ship was rekindled in modern times, thanks to numerous organizations, particularly Chicago's non-profit Christmas Ship Committee and the United States Coast Guard.

On the first Saturday in December, the time when the *Rouse Simmons* would have been selling its fragrant pine cargo near the Clark Street bridge, the new Christmas Tree Ship, with a Christmas tree attached to its masthead as the traditional announcement of its cargo, brings its load of Christmas happiness to Chicago's Navy Pier. The Coast Guard icebreaker *Mackinaw* beginning in 2000 until 2005, after which this World War Two ship was decommissioned and converted to a museum at Mackinaw City, Michigan, then the newly-launched Coast Guard ship *Mackinaw* from 2006 to 2010, and, now, since 2011, the new Coast Guard cut-

Over the past dozen years, a U.S. Coast Guard ship has revived the annual tradition of bringing Christmas trees to Chicago. The formal ceremonies at Navy Pier and the actual unloading of the trees attract hundreds of spectators. (PHOTOS BY CRIS KOHL)

ter *Alder,* with their crews of Coast Guard sailors (the popular "Coasties"), see to it that needy families will not have to do without a tree for their celebrations.

A formal ceremony commemorating lost Great Lakes sailors in general, and those who perished on the *Rouse Simmons* in particular, accompanies the annual visit of the new Christmas Tree Ship to Chicago. Officers from the Great Lakes Naval Training Center, the U.S. Coast Guard, the Chicago Marine Police, the Salvation Army, the Sea Scouts, naval cadets, and several other organizations, including yacht clubs, gather in front of Navy Pier's dramatic "Captain at the Helm" statue on the waterfront. (See color photos on pages 91-93.)

An Honor Guard of Shipmasters stands at attention before placing a memorial wreath at the base of the statue. A U.S. Coast Guard helicopter, carrying another wreath, flies overhead, hovers, dips its nose slightly as a salute to the statue representing all sailors lost at sea, then heads out to Lake Michigan's open waters and drops its wreath while the Great Lakes Naval Brass Band plays the Navy hymn.

Brief speeches by a representative of the Christmas Ship Committee, a Chicago city alderman, and the captain of the new Christmas Tree Ship are interspersed with nautical entertainment. Lee Murdock often plays his guitar and sings one or two of his songs that pertain to the Christmas Tree Ship -- the old and the new ones -- while standing at the microphone on a makeshift stage next to the captain's statue at Navy Pier. Ruth Fleswig Gibson often tells the tale of the great disappointment felt by her mother, when she was a little girl, when the Christmas Tree Ship failed to arrive in Chicago in 1912, the story that inspired Ruth to write a children's book about the ship (see color photos on page 94.)

Then the unloading of the 1,000 Christmas trees -- which were actually cut by "Coasties" from northern Michigan forests -- from the ship begins, manual labor performed by volunteer groups of mostly young people. Chicago's Christmas Ship Committee annually selects one major organization, such as the Salvation Army or the United Way, to arrange the distribution of the trees to needy families through a variety of smaller recipient organizations, such as churches and community social groups, and the trees are loaded onto their waiting trucks at Navy Pier.

The torch was passed and the U.S. Coast Guard generously accepted the mantle of Captain Schuenemann's legacy so that the Christmas Tree Ship tradition can continue.

Photo by Cris Kohl

TEN

The Legacy

It is amazing that a 100-year-old shipwreck in Lake Michigan has become the inspiration for a number of modern traditions of Christmas.

Dramatizations, concerts and musicals relating the story of the famous Christmas Tree Ship spring up every year just prior to Christmas in numerous Great Lakes locations ranging from Chicago to Door County, Wisconsin, to Bellevue, Ohio, keeping this dramatic yuletide tale alive. Audiences enjoy "The Christmas Schooner" by John Reeger and Julie Shannon, a musical play inspired by the *Rouse Simmons* story that Chris Jones of the *Chicago Tribune* described as "a show that reminds us of the oft-neglected maritime past of this community...." Great Lakes troubadour Lee Murdock has paid tribute to this beloved tale by composing songs that have become classics about the *Rouse Simmons* and the modern-day Christmas Tree Ship, the *"Mac."* Lee's annual Christmas Tree Ship concert is wildly popular.

Several fine books have singled out the *Rouse Simmons* and brought her story to the forefront. Authors Rochelle Pennington, Ruth Fleswig Gibson, and Fred Neuschel often appear before groups to speak movingly about the fabled ship, crew and the proud Schuenemann family. Great Lakes maritime artists Bob Heuel, Charles Vickery, James Andrews, and the newest addition to this talented group, Eric Forsberg, have produced many exquisite paintings of the *Rouse Simmons* that are highly prized by collectors. Their attention to detail -- wanting to get the image historically accurate -- as well as capturing the perfect mood is remarkable.

And the lost *Rouse Simmons* has been found. Divers have been to her grave and brought back pictures for all to see. When we speak to groups and show the amazing images of the skeletons that remain of the trees that were put there on the ship, with such hope, by Captain Schuenemann and his crew, the audiences literally gasp. The sight of the Christmas trees still there, piled up in the hold, brings this tragic story home to all of us, and makes the tale more real and even more touching.

What is it about the *Rouse Simmons* that has grabbed our imaginations? There are many other tragic shipwrecks in the Great Lakes and elsewhere, many with far greater loss of life. There were even other Christmas Tree Ships that sank, including the *S. Thal* that took her crew with her to the bottom. But the *Rouse Simmons* was special in the hearts of Chicagoans. Every year the front pages of the newspapers heralded the arrival of the much-loved, jovial Captain Santa and his schooner -- it was an event greatly anticipated and treasured. Everyone knew that ships sailing the lakes at the end of the shipping season were in danger and yet Captain Santa courageously fought the gales of November so that families might have their wonderful holiday experience to begin the festive season. When he lost that fight in 1912, that might have been the end of the interest, but what elevates the story to a different level is what happened after the ship was gone. The Schuenemann women did what was virtually unthinkable -- they determined to carry on the work -- that even though the beloved Captain Santa had been lost, his loving generosity of spirit would live on. At a time when women could not vote and rarely worked outside their homes, these remarkable women carried on in an industry that was completely a man's sphere. Women just didn't do that sort of thing. And they succeeded -- the public enthusiastically responded to the stalwart Mrs. Captain Santa and her brave daughters who persevered in the Schuenemann family tradition. Barbara and her girls believed in the course that Herman had set, they believed in the mission, and they earnestly felt that their husband and father would have wanted them to do whatever was necessary to make sure the children of Chicago would not be disappointed. If the story had ended with the loss of the Christmas Tree Ship and Captain Santa, it would have been an unmitigated tragedy, but the courage and indomitable spirit of Barbara, Elsie, Hazel and Pearl made it a heroic tale. They didn't just maintain the tradition of bringing Christmas to Chicago, they carried on the legacy of the generous, brave, heroic spirit of Captain Santa and his ship and crew.

The story of the *Rouse Simmons*, the famed Christmas Tree Ship, is the Great Lakes' unique entry in the catalogue of all things Christmas. Not only has this dramatic tale of toil and tragedy, love and charity, family and tradition, mourning and recovery, persisted -- it has captured, and continues to captivate in ever-increasing numbers with each passing year, the imaginations, the emotions and the appreciation of millions of people who live in the maritime-rich region of the inland seas.

The *Rouse Simmons*, the legendary Christmas Tree Ship, the symbol of loving and giving, still sails.

Photo by Cris Kohl

BIBLIOGRAPHY

PRIMARY SOURCES

Records of the Bureau of Marine Inspection and Navigation (Record Group 41), Milwaukee, Wisconsin, Licenses of Enrolled Vessels, 1853-1912. License of Enrolled Vessel for *Rouse Simmons*, August 27, 1868, vol. 87, p. 349.

Records of District Courts of the United States, (RG 21), Debtor's Petition filed by Herman E. Schuenemann on January 4, 1907, in the U. S. District Court, Chicago.

..............Otto Parker's Libel for seaman's wages filed on August 29, 1898, in the U. S. District Court, Milwaukee.

Records of the United States Coast Guard (Record Group 26), Life Saving Station Log, Kewaunee, Wisconsin, log entry for November 23, 1912, describing sighting the *Rouse Simmons* and reporting her distress to the crew at Two Rivers, Wisconsin, Life Saving Station.

..............Life Saving Station Log, Two Rivers, Wisconsin, log entry for November 23, 1912, describing the abortive rescue attempt for the *Rouse Simmons*.

NEWSPAPERS

Many issues of the following newspapers were used in the research for this book:

Chicago American	*Detroit News*	*Manitowoc Daily Herald*
Chicago Daily Journal	*Detroit Tribune*	*Milwaukee Daily News*
Chicago Daily News	*Door County* (Wisconsin)	*Milwaukee Journal*
Chicago Daily Tribune	*Advocate*	*Milwaukee Sentinel*
(Chicago) *Inter Ocean*	*Duluth Herald*	*Sturgeon Bay* (Wisconsin)
Chicago Record-Herald	*Duluth Evening Herald*	*Advocate*
Detroit Free Press	*Duluth News Tribune*	*Toledo Blade*

SECONDARY SOURCES: BOOKS

Behrend, Carl. *The Legend of the Christmas Tree Ship*. Munising, Michigan: Self-published, 2005.

Bowen, Dana Thomas. *Lore of the Lakes*. Daytona Beach, Florida: Self-published, 1940.

Boyer, Dwight. *Great Stories of the Great Lakes*. New York: Dodd, Mead & Company, 1966.

Brown, David G. *White Hurricane, A Great Lakes November Gale and America's Deadliest Maritime Disaster*. New York: McGraw-Hill, 2002.

Crane, Carol. *The Christmas Tree Ship*. Ann Arbor, Michigan: Sleeping Bear Press, 2011.

Creviere, Paul J., Jr. *Wild Gales and Tattered Sails*. Wisconsin: self-published, 1997.

Frese, Rita L., and David M. Young, eds., Chicago Maritime Society. *From Lumber Hook ers to the Hooligan Fleet, A Treasury of Chicago Maritime History.* Chicago Lake Claremont Press, 2008.

Greenwood, John O. *Namesakes 1910-1919.* Cleveland, Ohio: Freshwater Press, Inc. 1986.

Heden, Karl E. *Directory of Shipwrecks of the Great Lakes.* Boston: Bruce Humphries Publishers, 1966.

Hirthe, Walter M. and Mary K. *Schooner Days in Door County.* Minneapolis, MN: Voya geur Press, 1986.

Karamanski, Theodore J. *Schooner Passage, Sailing Ships and the Lake Michigan Fron tier.* Detroit: Wayne State University Press, in association with the Chicago Mari time Society, 2000.

Kohl, Cris. *The 100 Best Great Lakes Shipwrecks, Volume I.* West Chicago: Seawolf Com munications, Inc., 1998; revised edition 2005.

............*The Great Lakes Diving Guide,* West Chicago, Illinois: Seawolf Communications Inc., revised and enlarged edition 2008.

Kohl, Cris, and Joan Forsberg. *Shipwrecks at Death's Door.* West Chicago: Seawolf Com munications, Inc., 2007.

Miall, Antony and Peter. *The Victorian Christmas Book.* London: J. M. Dent & Sons 1978.

Morris, Desmond. *Christmas Watching.* London: Jonathan Cape, 1992.

Neuschel, Fred. *August and Herman Schuenemann, Tree Captains of Lake Michigan.* Self published, Algoma, Wisconsin, 1993.

............*Lives and Legends of the Christmas Tree Ships.* Ann Arbor, Michigan: The Uni versity of Michigan Press, 2007.

Pennington, Rochelle M. *The Christmas Tree Ship, The Story of Captain Santa.* Woodruff Wisconsin: The Guest Cottage, Inc., dba Amherst Press, 2002.

............*The Historic Christmas Tree Ship, A True Story of Faith, Hope and Love.* Wiscon sin: Pathways Press, 2004.

Pitz, Herbert. *Lake Michigan Disasters.* Manitowoc, Wisconsin: 1925, reprinted Manito woc Maritime Museum, no date.

Quaife, Milo M. *Lake Michigan.* New York and Indianapolis: The Bobbs-Merrill Com pany, 1944.

Ratigan, William. *Great Lakes Shipwrecks and Survivals.* Grand Rapids, Michigan: Wm B. Eerdmans Publishing Company, 1960.

Snyder, Phillip. *The Christmas Tree Book.* New York: The Viking Press, 1976.

............*December 25th, The Joys of Christmas Past.* New York: Dodd, Mead & Com pany, 1985.

Wagenknecht, Edward, ed. *A Fireside Book of Yuletide Tales.* New York: The Bobbs-Mer rill Company, 1948.

Young, David M. *Chicago Maritime, An Illustrated History.* DeKalb, Illinois: Norther Illinois University Press, 2001.

PERIODICAL LITERATURE

Blahnik, Mary. "Story of the Christmas Tree Ship." *Shipwreck Journal,* Vol. 13, No. 4 (Winter, 1996-97), 1, 6-8.

Brazer, Marjorie Cahn. "The Christmas Tree Ship." *Great Lakes Travel and Living.* (December, 1986), 21-22.

Charrney, Theodore S. *Commemorating the Fiftieth Anniversary of the Loss of the Schooner Rouse Simmons.* Chicago: Self-published, 1962.

............"The Loss of the *Rouse Simmons.*" *Soundings* (Newsletter of the Wisconsin Marine Historical Society), Vol. 4, No. 2 (Winter 1963-64).

............"The *Rouse Simmons* and the Port of Chicago." *Inland Seas,* Vol. 43, Number 4 (Winter, 1987), 242-246.

The Christmas Tree Ship: *Rouse Simmons.*" *Southport* (Newsletter of the Kenosha County Historical Society), Vol. 76, No. 3 (Winter, 2003), n. n.

Harrison, Gene C. "The Christmas Tree Ship." *Milwaukee Yacht Club Log* (November-December, 1984), 1-2.

Hollister, Fred. "Loss of the Christmas Tree Schooner." *Sea Classics,* Vol. 10, No. 1 (January, 1977), 6-11, 82.

Kohl, Cris. "The Christmas Tree Wreck." *Wreck Diving Magazine.* Issue 4, 2004, 8-15.

............"Great Lakes Schooners." *Scuba Diving Magazine.* Vol. 14, No. 9, Issue 132 (October, 2005), 33-38, 96.

Kuhns, Roger. "The Risky Careers of Christmas Schooner Captains." *Door County Living.* (Fall/Winter, 2003), 10-13.

Longacre, Glenn V. "The Christmas Tree Ship: Captain Herman E. Schuenemann and the Schooner *Rouse Simmons.*" *Prologue,* Vol. 38, No. 4 (Winter, 2006), U.S. National Archives and Records Administration.

Marine Review, The. "Schooner *Rouse Simmons.*" Feb., 1913, 74.

Neuschel, Fred. "November 23, 1912: The Rest of the Story." *Anchor News,* Vol. 21, No. 1 and 3 (January-February and May-June, 1990), 4-11 and 44-52.

Nowak, Joseph A., Jr. "The Christmas Tree Schooner *Rouse Simmons.*" *Sea History.* (Winter, 1987-88), 40-41.

Pourchot, Mary Ellen. "The Christmas Tree Ship." *American History Illustrated.* Vol. XVII, Number 8 (December, 1982), 11-13.

Sander, Phil. "Christmas Tree Ship." *Kenosha Ramblings.* 1991, 69-71.

Sarrett, Vincent. "Christmases Remembered." *Gourmet* Magazine (December, 1966), 24-26.

Walther, Gary. "The German Tree in America." *American History Illustrated.* Vol. XVII, Number 8 (December, 1982), 15-17.

VIDEO / DVD / CD

Kohl, Cris, and Joan Forsberg. "Deep Shipwrecks of the Great Lakes." Seawolf Communications, Inc., 2009.

............"Shipwreck Tales of Chicago." Seawolf Communications, Inc., 2012.

INDEX

Words in *italics* denote a ship's name.
A number in **bold** denotes a photograph or a drawing on that page.

ABOUT THE AUTHORS

Cris Kohl and Joan Forsberg, well-known maritime historians, scuba divers, photographers, videographers, authors, and lecturers, are a husband-and-wife team who love to explore shipwrecks, particularly those in the Great Lakes. They both have university degrees in History and underwater archaeology certifications from Great Britain's Nautical Archaeology Society (NAS).

Joan, from Chicago, has been the Chairman of the Shipwrecks and Our Maritime Heritage Room at Chicago's annual "Our World -- Underwater" Show since 1996. She is the author of the scuba celebrity cook-and-tell book, *Diver's Guide to the Kitchen,* and articles in magazines such as *Immersed, Great Lakes Boating,* and *Wreck Diving* (for which she serves as Copy Editor). Joan appears behind the camera shooting underwater video, and in front of the camera as Cris' underwater model. In her three terms as President of the Underwater Archaeological Society of Chicago (2008, 2009, 2010), she spearheaded several significant maritime history projects. She is the recipient of the 2011 UASC Award "for many years of leadership and dedication." Joan was inducted into the international Women Divers Hall of Fame in 2010, and she is currently an elected Trustee of WDHOF.

Photo by Lynn Funkhouser

Cris, a prize-winning underwater photographer with a Master's Degree in History, is from Windsor, Ontario. He served on the Executive Board of the Ontario Underwater Council for nine years (1988-1997), is a Past President of the Underwater Archaeological Society of Chicago (2004), and has written twelve books and more than 300 magazine and newsletter articles about Great Lakes shipwrecks. For ten years, several dozen of his shipwreck articles appeared regularly in Canada's *DIVER Magazine.* His work has been published in every issue of the international publication, *Wreck Diving Magazine,* since it began operations in 2003. He has helped locate and identify several shipwrecks in the Great Lakes. He is the 2008 recipient of the annual "Our World -- Underwater" Outstanding Achievement Award. His most recent book is the expanded *The Great Lakes Diving Guide,* the most comprehensive book ever published about Great Lakes shipwrecks.

Both have appeared on numerous television programs, including on the History Channel, the Discovery Channel, and Chicago's WTTW and CBS. Co-authors of the recent book, *Shipwrecks at Death's Door,* co-editors of the 2010 book, *Our World -- Underwater: The First 40 Years,* and producers of a dozen history documentaries about Great Lakes shipwrecks (available on widescreen DVD), Cris and Joan are currently working on more shipwreck book collaborations.

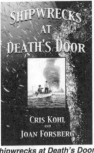

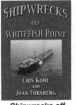

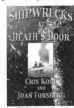